Our Town

Our Town

Images and
Stories
from the
Museum of the
City of
New York

INTRODUCTION BY

Robert R. Macdonald

ESSAYS BY

Hilton Als

Louis Auchincloss

Arthur and Barbara Gelb

Oscar Hijuelos

Caroline Rennolds Milbank

Elizabeth Barlow Rogers

Robert A. M. Stern
with Thomas Mellins

HARRY N. ABRAMS, INC.,
PUBLISHERS

Library of Congress Cataloging-in-
Publication Data
Our town : images and stories from the
Museum of the City of New York
/ introduction by Robert R. Macdonald;
essays by Hilton Als . . . [et al.].
p.   cm.
Includes bibliographical references and
index.
ISBN 0-8109-3698-4 (Abrams).—
ISBN 0-910961-09-3 (Museum)
1. New York (N.Y.)—Civilization—Pictorial
works. 2. New York (N.Y.)—History—
Pictorial works. 3. New York (N.Y.)—
Civilization—Anecdotes. 4. New York
(N.Y.)—History—Anecdotes. I. Als,
Hilton, II. Museum of the City of New
York.
F128.37.O87   1997
974.7'1—DC21   97–20742

The Garden Party copyright © 1997 by
Hilton Als
Society in New York copyright © 1997 by
Louis Auchincloss
Eugene O'Neill's New York copyright
© 1997 by Arthur and Barbara Gelb
NY—Memoryville copyright © 1997 by
Oscar Hijuelos
Capturing the Ephemeral copyright © 1997
by Caroline Rennolds Milbank
How I Became a New Yorker copyright
© 1997 by Elizabeth Barlow Rogers
New York: American Architectural Center
copyright © 1997 by Robert A. M. Stern

The publication of
Our Town: Images and Stories from the
Museum of the City of New York
is partially supported by a generous grant
from the Vincent Astor Foundation.

Produced by Constance Sullivan Books, Ltd.

Printed and bound in Hong Kong

Published in 1997 by Harry N. Abrams,
Incorporated, New York. All rights
reserved. No part of the contents of this
book may be reproduced without the written permission of the publisher

Harry N. Abrams, Inc.
100 Fifth Avenue
New York, N.Y. 10011
www.abramsbooks.com

The Museum of the City of New York is a
non-profit, private educational agency
established in 1923 to collect, preserve, and
present original materials related to the
history of New York City. In addition to
individual contributions and gifts from
foundations and corporations, the Museum
receives public funds from the New York
State Council on the Arts, the National
Endowment for the Humanities, and federal agencies. The City of New York, the
Museum building's owner, provides support
in the form of operating and programmatic
funds through the Department of Cultural
Affairs.

MUSEUM OF
MC
THE CITY OF
NY
NEW YORK

Museum of the City of New York
1220 Fifth Avenue
New York, New York 10029
212.534.1672
www.mcny.org

frontispiece:
Attributed to Augustine Herrman

New Amsterdam (The Montanus View),
c. 1650
Copper engraving
Harris D. Colt, L231.2

Established as a fur- and timber-trading
post in 1624 by the Dutch West India
Company, New Amsterdam quickly became
a diverse settlement focused on international commerce. By 1660, a hubbub of
languages—eighteen in all—filled the
town, and the citizens practiced a variety
of religions—although only the Calvinists
could worship in public. In 1664, the English, who by then controlled the surrounding colonies, demanded New Amsterdam's
surrender and the inhabitants offered no
resistance. Though the Dutch recaptured
New Amsterdam briefly in 1667, they
willingly exchanged it for the sugar-rich
British colony of Surinam. Under the
English, New Amsterdam was renamed
New York; but the island on which the
town stood has always been called Manhattan, a name that probably derives from
a Munsee Indian word for the place.

Contents

Preface 7
Rudolph W. Giuliani

Introduction 9
Robert R. Macdonald

Acknowledgments and photography credits 15

Society in New York 33
Louis Auchincloss

NY—Memoryville 36
Oscar Hijuelos

The Garden Party 40
Hilton Als

Capturing the Ephemeral 43
Caroline Rennolds Milbank

How I Became a New Yorker 46
Elizabeth Barlow Rogers

Eugene O'Neill's New York 203
Arthur and Barbara Gelb

New York: American Architectural Center 208
Robert A.M. Stern with Thomas Mellins

Index of Illustrations 216

I love New York and would not want to live anyplace else. I have traveled all over the world and been to almost every country. I have lived in Hawaii, Santo Domingo, China, Istanbul, France, and Italy, to name a few.

However, I still think New York offers you more than you could possibly want. Anything that you are interested in you can find here—music, art, museums, theater, funny odd places to go, all sorts of little places to visit, restaurants of every ethnic group and so many other diversions. All of that, and of course the reason that is best of all is, there are so many different types of people that you can have as friends.

Brooke Astor

Preface

Rudolph W. Giuliani
Mayor
The City of New York

On May 4, 1897, Manhattan, the Bronx, Brooklyn, Queens, and Staten Island joined together to sign the charter of Greater New York, consolidating the five boroughs into the City of New York. Each borough entered this historic alliance as an independent city or county but had the foresight and wisdom to realize that they were all integrally linked together. From City Island to Coney Island, Forest Hills to Turtle Bay, and Tremont to Tottenville, New York City became the most extensive and populous city in the country, and the financial and cultural capital of the world.

Through three-quarters of a century, the Museum of the City of New York has gathered a collection of more than 1.5 million items dating from our earliest days as a Dutch colony to the 1990s, to help us learn about our city's rich and fascinating past.

What better way to celebrate both the Museum's seventy-fifth anniversary and the centennial of the consolidation of New York City than with the publication of *Our Town, Images and Stories from the Museum of the City of New York*, a tribute to this world-class cultural institution whose collections trace the four-hundred-year history of our five boroughs?

Today, the Museum's fine holdings include paintings, maps, photographs, theater and military memorabilia, costumes, manuscripts, and toys. As a life-long New Yorker, I can appreciate such unique treasures as Mayor Fiorello La Guardia's smoking jacket and a genuine Checker cab!

The extraordinary variety and abundance of the Museum's fine collections make us proud to be New Yorkers and to reaffirm the vital partnership between the Museum and the people of New York City. This special partnership blossomed in 1923, when a group of business and civic leaders established the Museum of the City of New York in Gracie Mansion to collect, preserve, and present the city's history. By 1932, the collections had grown so large that the Museum moved to more spacious quarters in a new Georgian Revival building on upper Fifth Avenue, now a designated landmark.

Our administration has worked closely with the Museum to provide the support it needs to grow and flourish, because without our museums and cultural institutions, New York simply wouldn't be the capital of the world. In partnership with the Museum, the City—through the Department of Cultural Affairs —is providing capital support for the design and reconstruction of the building.

The "Museum for a New Century" will feature environmentally controlled galleries to protect the priceless collections, and newly designed, state-of-the-art learning and research centers to serve the people of New York City into the new millennium.

Our Town, Images and Stories from the Museum of the City of New York is a celebration of a cultural institution that not only preserves the history, life, and diversity of our five boroughs but also illuminates the spirit, energy, and creativity that make New York the greatest city on earth.

Introduction

Robert R. Macdonald
Director
Museum of the City of New York

I like to see a man proud of the place in which he lives. I like to see a man live so that his place will be proud of him. — ABRAHAM LINCOLN

These words, attributed to Abraham Lincoln and inscribed in stone and wood at the entrance to the Museum of the City of New York and above the Museum's beautiful marble spiral staircase, capture the ideals on which America's first museum about a city was founded. Inspired by the Musée Carnavalet in Paris, a diverse group of New Yorkers led by Henry Collins Brown, whose historical vignettes about the City had been appearing in *Valentine's Manual* since 1917, established the Museum of the City of New York on July 17, 1923. Their purpose was, "To do all things necessary, fit or suitable to create a love for and interest in all things pertaining to the City of New York."

The Museum's first home was Gracie Mansion, an early nineteenth-century farmhouse located on the East River below Hell Gate, and today the official residence of the mayor of New York City. The Parks Department, which had owned the house since 1896, made it available to the Museum, and the doors were opened to the public on November 7, 1924. The prospect of creating a great museum dedicated to America's Empire City soon attract-ed prominent businessmen, financiers, and politicians. The most active of them, the prestigious banker James Speyer, was to guide the Museum throughout its formative years.

Henry Collins Brown, who served as the Museum's founding director, was viewed as too antiquarian by Speyer and other trustees, and he was replaced in 1926 by Hardinge Scholle, who held the position for twenty-five years. Scholle, who had trained at the Art Institute of Chicago, made it his first task to organize a major exhibition at the Fine Arts Building on West Fifty-seventh Street. Titled *Old New York*, the exhibition featured loans from prominent families and included furniture, silver, photographs, theater memorabilia, costumes, toys, marine collectibles, and prints. A huge success, the show drew almost twenty thousand visitors in its nine-day run.

The popularity of *Old New York* convinced James Speyer and the other trustees that a permanent home for their museum was needed, and in 1927 the Museum entered into an agreement with the City of New York: the City would provide land on Fifth Avenue for a new building; on their part, the trustees would raise $2 million in private funds to construct it and then donate it to the City. The money was quickly raised in gifts and pledges, and on April 30, 1929—the 140th anniversary of the inauguration of George Washington in New York as the first president of the United States—the cor-nerstone was laid for the new building designed by Joseph H. Freedlander. At the ceremony, the former governor of New York and recent presidential candidate Al Smith commented,

I feel very proud of the fact that I was somewhat instrumental in doing my share, resulting in the present plans for the erection of the Museum of the City of New York. I had the pleasure and the very great honor of signing the bill, giving it a special incorporation, and at that time . . . I was familiar with the objects to be accomplished by the erection of this Museum. I like to think of the very great pleasure that it will give not only to our own people but to the many visitors to our city from all over the world. I particularly like to think of it as an institution for the promotion of education.

Mayor Jimmy Walker laid the cornerstone, and the Museum was dedicated, "For all the people of New York and Strangers within her Gates." Almost six months to the day later, the New York stock market crashed, ushering in the Great Depression. The immediate consequence for the Museum was that the construction project ran out of funds, and in the end only half of the architect's original plan was realized. After twenty months of construction, the partially completed Georgian Revival building opened to the public, on January 11, 1932.

From its inception, the Museum of the City of New York has relied on the generosity of New Yorkers. The first major gift was made by the real-estate magnate J. Clarence Davies, who donated fifteen thousand prints, photographs, and books. But if the Museum of the City of New York relied on donors to assemble what today is a world renowned collection, it also relied on three extraordinary women to build and shape those collections into a great historical treasury: Grace M. Mayer, May Davenport Seymour, and V. Isabelle Miller.

For twenty-nine years, from 1930 to 1959, Grace Mayer presided over the Museum's photographic and print collections, gathering such treasures as the Harry T. Peters collection of Currier & Ives prints and the photographic work of Berenice Abbott, Jacob A. Riis, and the Byron Company, as well as prints by Reginald Marsh and Childe Hassam. May Davenport Seymour, the daughter of a noted theatrical producer, established America's most important theater collection, which ranges from original manuscripts by playwright Eugene O'Neill to more than three thousand theater costumes dating from the mid-nineteenth century. V. Isabelle Miller quietly and diligently secured a collection of New York furniture and silver that is among the finest such assemblages in the United States. Coincidentally Miss Miller and Miss Seymour each worked at the Museum for thirty-seven years, retiring in 1963.

Gathering New York's historic patrimony was only one part of fulfilling the Museum's mission. As Al Smith observed, the Museum provided the City with a new educational resource. In 1935, Luke Vincent Lockwood, chairman of the Committee on Education reported,

The educational value of the exhibitions themselves is furthered and clarified by the Department of Education, which begins in the Museum but extends far beyond the Museum walls. Sunday lectures, which are free to the public, deal with topics, contemporary or historical, which concern the life and activities of the City. For the children, there are games based on special features of the exhibits, studies in local history and municipal government, and portable history groups which are lent to the schools. For teachers and other interested persons, there are college courses in the study of Museum Methods and Practice in Social Studies, courses which fit them to explain the exhibitions and to guide groups more intelligently.

Lockwood went on to describe the Museum's self-guided walking tours, called "Trips and Trails," and curriculum kits on such topics as the history of New York's water supply, transportation, fire control, and education. By 1939, the Museum was annually serving more than 250,000 students through guided tours and outreach programs.

Many of the Museum's public programs were curtailed during World War II; however, the curators continued to build the collections by interesting a multitude of New Yorkers in donating their treasures. From the start, superb dioramas depicting historic scenes in the life of the City had been a major attraction, and in the 1940s the Museum began to present special temporary exhibitions with such titles as *Dining in Old New York, Silver by New York Makers, Coney Island—Playground of the World, Those Elegant New Yorkers—250 Years of Fashion*, and *New York Street Scenes—1852*. In the mid-1950s, two dynamic women, Janet Pinney and Susan Lyman, broke new ground when they established a now-famous gallery, called "Please Touch." Here visitors, particularly the young, were encouraged to touch artifacts of New York's everyday life, such as lanterns, andirons, and woodworking planes. The Museum's educational techniques were emulated by institutions throughout the country; indeed, entire museums have been created specifically around the "Please Touch" concept.

In 1951, Hardinge Scholle retired as director and was replaced by John Walden Myer, who had served as assistant director for eighteen years. Myer was followed in 1958 by K. Ross Toole, whose tenure lasted only two years. In 1960, Ralph Miller, who had served as assistant director since 1951, was appointed the Museum's fourth director. During his tenure, the Museum launched its popular walking-tour series with the guidance of Henry Hope Reed, Jr. Ambitious exhibitions such as *New York, the Scene, On Stage, 1913–1963*, and the memorable *Dutch Gallery* brought increased attention to the Museum.

In 1966, the noted author and attorney Louis Auchincloss was elected the Museum's president, a position he held for twenty-four years. Speaking of history in general, Auchincloss suggested that New York's own museum could play an even more important role in the lives of its citizens: "To me one of the dimensions of life is missing in any human being who knows nothing of the history of the area in which he lives. The man who resides in Manhattan and has a comprehensive knowledge of American history and culture, but who is entirely ignorant of the Dutch and English periods of his island, who knows nothing of New York in the Revolution, the Civil War, or World War I, strikes me as having an arid corner in the garden of his intellect." It was during Louis Auchincloss's presidency that Joseph Veach Noble moved from the Metropolitan Museum of Art to become the Museum's fifth director. Together, Auchincloss and Noble brought new purpose and excitement to the institution. A fund-raising drive ensued, and Noble presented two revolutionary exhibitions, one on drugs and the other on venereal disease. Both attracted large audiences, as did *Cityrama*, a multimedia history of New York City created by Noble. Later *Cityrama* was updated and given the title *The Big Apple*. As the Museum celebrated its fiftieth anniversary in 1973, there was hope that a new era for the venerable institution had begun.

Despite the valiant efforts of the trustees and staff, however, the financial crises that plagued New York City during the 1970s prevented the Museum of the City of New York from achieving many of its goals. So, when I was named director of the Museum in 1985, upon Noble's retirement, having previously directed history museums in Pennsylvania, Connecticut, and Louisiana, I initiated a consultant-assisted review of every aspect of the Museum's operations. Based on this extensive analysis, a strategic plan for the Museum was drafted. In September 1987, the Board of Trustees adopted "A Museum for A New Century," which set out an ambitious blueprint for the Museum's future. The plan was founded on a reaffirmation of the institution's mission as a history museum.

Under "A Museum for A New Century," the Museum's staff was reorganized and expanded, and a series of special historical exhibitions on such diverse subjects as homelessness, the history of Broadway, Greenwich Village as a center of counterculture, and the Irish in New York were presented, accompanied by educational programs for youth, adult, school, family, and scholarly audiences. The Museum launched its publications program with the presentation of *On Being Homeless: Historical Perspectives*. Modern techniques for the management and care of cultural collections were applied within the museum's various departments, and a digitized electronic data base was created that made the collections available to a global audience on the Museum's World Wide Web site. Since 1987, more than eighty special exhibitions have been created, some of which have traveled to other museums in the United States and in Europe. In 1990, the Museum organized the New York City History Fair to serve students and teachers in each of the City's five boroughs. This event has grown to be the largest urban-history fair in the United States.

The most ambitious element of "A Museum for A New Century" was the restoration and completion of the Museum's Fifth Avenue premises. The noted architect James Stewart Polshek was engaged to develop a plan for a new six-story wing, which would more than double the exhibition, educational, and research spaces. Ralph Appelbaum, one of the country's leading exhibition designers, worked with the Museum staff to plan exhibitions for the now world-class history museum about New York City.

In 1990, after serving for nearly a quarter-century as the Museum's president, Louis Auchincloss was elected chairman, and David C. Clapp became the Museum's president. Under their leadership, the Museum has launched a capital campaign to raise public and private funds for "A Museum for A New Century."

As the Museum of the City of New York looks back on seventy-five years of service to the people of New York and the nation, it can take pride in the men and women who have worked so diligently in gathering the Museum's magnificent collections and using them to tell the many stories of one of the world's most extraordinary cities. Building on that tradition of service, the Museum looks forward to the new millennium and to addressing the need of New Yorkers to understand the ever-changing dynamics of their special community. It is the same mission the Museum's founders articulated in 1923, when they chose the words of Abraham Lincoln to express their vision of the Museum's role in the life of their city.

This book,

commemorating the

75th anniversary

of the

Museum of the City

of New York,

is dedicated to

Louis S. Auchincloss.

Acknowledgments

Peter Simmons
Chair, Publications Committee
Museum of the City of New York

Our Town, conceived by Robert R. Macdonald, Director of the Museum of the City of New York, and produced in a year's time, owes its success to the invaluable contributions of many individuals. The project was fueled by the professionalism, enthusiasm, and tireless determination of Constance Sullivan, whose impeccable aesthetic discretion meshed with sound business direction to maximize the book's potential. The staff at the Museum of the City of New York, in particular Joanna Ellwood, Collections Associate, toiled to maintain strict schedules for image selection, photography, manuscript preparation, and editing. Jan Ramirez, Deputy Director for Programs and Collections, fine-tuned the images selected from the Museum's boundless collections, and Kathy Benson, the Museum's Head of Education, single-handedly composed the narrative captions out of gleanings from a multitude of curatorial and exhibition files. Every word of the text was professionally scrutinized by Ellyn Allison, who brought fluidity to the work in addition to grammatical accuracy. Katy Homans' superior design blended images and text into a beautiful book, and Robert Hennessey guided the printing of the book's forty-seven duotones. At Harry N. Abrams, the project was handled with finesse by Marti Malovany.

Of course, *Our Town* would not be here today without the generous financial support of the Vincent Astor Foundation, whose contributions toward preserving and stimulating the arts have helped make New York City the greatest subject matter on earth. Ultimately, the success of *Our Town* lies in the unparalleled collections of the Museum of the City of New York, which have been carefully acquired, documented, exhibited, and conserved for seventy-five years.

PHOTOGRAPHY CREDITS
With few exceptions, the photography in *Our Town* is the work of two photographers who work closely with the Museum of the City of New York, Arthur Vitols of Helga Studio, and Victor Petryakov. The silver pieces on page 26 and page 29 (top) were photographed by John Parnell, the gaming table on page 74 is by Bruce M. White, the Stettheimer Doll House photographs on pages 146–47 are by Lynton Gardiner, and the painting on page 199 is courtesy of the Schmidt Bingham Gallery.

John Wollaston (active 1736–1767)

Mary Spratt Provoost Alexander
(Mrs. James Alexander), c. 1750
Oil on canvas
Gift of William Hamilton Russell,
50.215.4

The English painter, John Wollaston had been a successful portraitist in his homeland before he arrived in New York in 1749. His paintings were soon in demand, not only in New York, where he worked until 1752, but also in Maryland, Virginia, and Pennsylvania. During the decade he spent in America, Wollaston painted about three hundred portraits. His subjects included many members of America's most prominent families, among them Mary Spratt Provoost Alexander and her husband, James Alexander, attorney general for the Province of New York from 1721 to 1723. Wollaston's sophisticated style elevated his patrons' taste and strongly influenced the work of contemporary painters, such as Benjamin West.

Attributed to Gerardus Duyckinck I
(1695–c. 1746)

Moses Levy, 1720–28
Oil on canvas
Bequest of Alphonse H. Kursheedt,
36.343.1

Attributed to Gerardus Duyckinck I
(1695–c. 1746)

Grace Mears Levy (Mrs. Moses
Levy), 1720–28
Oil on canvas
Bequest of Alphonse H. Kursheedt,
36.343.2

There are several rich and respect-
able families of Jews in New York;
and as they have equal rights with
every other citizen in the United
States, they suffer under no invidious
distinctions.
—John Lambert, *Travels through Canada*
and the United States . . . In the Years 1806,
1807, 1808, London, 1814

At the time these portraits were
painted, New York's small but influential Jewish community comprised
about seventy-five families, many of
whom were merchants. Moses Levy
was a prominent member of the
community and of the congregation
of Shearith Israel ("Remnant of
Israel"), the first Jewish congregation in North America.

Probably born in Germany, Moses
Levy arrived in New York from
London about 1695, became a successful trader and real-estate inves-
tor, and owned a fleet of merchant
ships. He was married twice, first
to Richa Asher and then, in 1718,
to Grace Mears. After Moses Levy
died in 1728, his wife opened a retail
shop in New York.

Ralph Earl (1751–1801)

Elizabeth Schuyler Hamilton, 1787
Oil on canvas
Gift of Mrs. Alexander Hamilton
and General Pierpont Morgan
Hamilton, 71.31.2

In 1787, when she was thirty years
old, Elizabeth Schuyler Hamilton
had her portrait painted by Ralph
Earl, a promising artist who had
been thrown into debtors' prison
for his inability to repay a modest
loan. A charming man, Earl had
secured the support of the Society
for the Relief of Distressed Debtors,
and several New York members
of the recently formed organization, including Elizabeth Schuyler
Hamilton, helped him by sitting for
their portraits at the prison where
he was incarcerated.

Alonzo Chappel (1828–1887)

*Alexander Hamilton as an Officer in
the Revolutionary Army*
Oil on canvas
Gift of Mrs. Alexander Hamilton
and General Pierpont Morgan
Hamilton, 71.31.5

In March 1776, Alexander Hamilton
was commissioned a captain of artil-
lery in the Provincial Company of
New York and later fought with dis-
tinction in the Continental Army at
the battles of Trenton and Princeton. His marriage to Elizabeth
Schuyler in 1780 brought him connections with one of New York
State's most powerful families.
Later in life, Hamilton served as a
delegate both to the Continental
Congress (1782–83) and to the
Constitutional Convention (1787),

and in 1789 he became the first
United States Secretary of the
Treasury. This distinguished patriot
and statesman lost his life in a duel
with his bitter political rival Aaron
Burr fought at Weehawken, New
Jersey, in 1804. More than fifty
years later, the artist Alonzo
Chappel executed this painting of
Hamilton, relying on earlier por-
traits of his subject and other
Revolutionary War soldiers for the
details of his unique depiction.

Attributed to Gilbert Stuart
(c. 1787–1813)

George Washington
Oil on canvas
Gift of James Speyer, 31.227

James Speyer was elected a trustee
of the Museum of the City of
New York in November 1923, four
months after its incorporation, and
he remained until his death in 1941
one of the institution's most influential supporters. In a notable gesture
of confidence and generosity,
he presented this unusual three-
quarter length portrait of General
George Washington to the fledgling
museum on the occasion of the 1932
opening of its new building.

Open robe, 1789
White silk satin Spitalfields brocade
(the motif dates from the mid-
1760s)
Gift of Mrs. Henry Wheeler de
Forest in memory of her husband,
54.209ab

Court suit, 1780s
Deep purple silk velvet elaborately
floral embroidered with silk floss
Gift of E. Coster Wilmerding,
50.256a-h

The white silk satin brocade gown
and deep-purple velvet suit shown
here were worn to the ball and
entertainment given on May 7,
1789, by the subscribers to the New
York Dancing Assembly in honor
of the inauguration of George
Washington as president of the
United States a few days before.
The gala was held in the ballroom
of the City Tavern.

Artist unknown

Justina Brandly Lasarus Isaacs
(Mrs. Joshua Isaacs), c. 1795
Oil on canvas
Bequest of Alma H. Harwood,
63.115.2

Rembrandt Peale (1778–1860)

Johanna Stoutenburgh Hone
(Mrs. John Hone)
Gift of Mrs. Philip A. Means in
memory of Frederic Giraud Foster,
65.72.2

Johanna Stoutenburgh Hone (1765–1838) was the sister-in-law of Philip Hone, a mayor of New York while Peale was in residence there. Rembrandt Peale was one of several sons of Maryland artist Charles Willson Peale who were named for great artists of the past and who pursued careers as painters. (Other Peale brothers were named Raphaelle, Rubens, and Titian.) Rembrandt spent seven years of his working life in New York, where he helped to found the National Academy of Design in 1826.

(Top) Artist unknown

Maria Burritt Cowdrey (Mrs. Peter Anderson Cowdrey), c. 1830
Portrait miniature, watercolor on ivory
Anonymous gift, 40.192

(Center) Ezra Ames (1768–1836)

Catherine Clinton Van Cortlandt (Mrs. Pierre Van Cortlandt, Jr.), c. 1800
Portrait miniature, watercolor on ivory
Bequest of Joseph B. Brenauer, 46.229.11

(Bottom) Artist unknown

Elias Braman, Jr.
Portrait miniature, watercolor on ivory
Gift of Miss Julie A. Ripley, 48.76

Like the snapshot of today, the portrait miniature of former times served as a keepsake, preserving forever fresh in the mind of its owner the features of an admired or beloved person. Miniatures were designed to be carried on the person or set into a small personal article such as a snuffbox or memorandum case. In the eighteenth century, it became the practice to tuck a lock of the sitter's hair and perhaps a snippet of handwriting from a letter into the back of the frame.

Evacuation Day jug

Probably New York City, 1783–1820
Salt-glazed stoneware with cobalt
decoration
Gift of Mr. Charles A. Dana, Jr.,
82.130

At the end of the Revolutionary
War, New York City was the last
official outpost held by the British.
On November 25, 1783—known
from then on as Evacuation Day—
all remaining British forces de-
parted from the United States. A
boisterous ten-day celebration followed, and for more than a century
thereafter New Yorkers commemo-
rated the end of the war in their
city with parades and patriotic
events. The centennial of Evacuation Day was one of the great civic
celebrations of the nineteenth
century in New York City. After
World War I, the holiday was
observed only once, in 1983, the
bicentennial year.

Gerrit Onckelbag (baptized
1670—died 1732)

Brandywine bowl, 1700—1720
Silver
Bequest of Charlotte A. Van
Cortlandt, 72.88.1

Cornelius Kierstede (1674—1757)

Tankard, 1700—1720
Silver
Gift of Mrs. Augustus Van
Cortlandt, 73.25

Fall-front desk (writing cabinet)
Flushing, New York, 1690–1720
Red cedar, white cedar, walnut,
lightwood inlays; tulip-poplar
Museum·purchase, Mrs. Elon
Huntington Hooker Fund,
45.112a-c

Attributed to the shop of Marinus
Willett and Jonathan Pearsee (active
together 1763–c. 1775)

Card table, 1763–75
Mahogany; oak, whitewood, pine
Bequest of Virginia T. Nicholas,
71.72

Side chair
New York, 1765–75
Mahogany; tulip-poplar corner
blocks and slip-seat frame
Gift of Mrs. Screven Lorillard, from
the collection of her mother, Mrs. J.
Insley Blair, 53.150.19

Attributed to John Wesley Jarvis
(1780–1840)

Philip Hone, 1820
Oil on canvas
Gift of Henry W. Munroe, 85.205.1

During his tenure as mayor of New York City in 1826–27, Philip Hone (1780–1851) presided over the opening of the Erie Canal and entertained the Marquis de Lafayette. After leaving office, Hone began the diary for which he is best known—a fascinating record of the city's political and social life that he kept until his death. In an 1827 entry, Hone made two observations about New York that are as true today as they were 170 years ago: "The spirit of pulling down and building up is abroad. The whole of New York is rebuilt about once in ten years. . . . Our good city of New York has already arrived at the state of society to be found in large cities of Europe. . . . where the two extremes of costly luxury and improvident waste are presented in daily and hourly contrast with squalid misery and hopeless destitution."

Robert Fulton (1765–1815)

Self-Portrait, 1800
Oil on canvas
Gift of Mrs. Frederick C. Hodgdon,
41.425

The inventor, engineer, and painter Robert Fulton is best known today as the builder, in 1807, of the *North River Steamboat.* The first commercially successful passenger steamboat in the world, the vessel received its popular name, *Clermont,* after Fulton's death. In 1814, the Fulton Ferry began regular service between Manhattan and Brooklyn, giving rise to Fulton Streets on either side of the East River.

Fulton was a fledgling artist when he painted this portrait.

Simon A. Bayley (active 1784–1799)

Cake basket, 1790–95
Silver
Gift of George Elsworth
Dunscombe, 32.237.6

Myer Myers (1723–1795)

Coffeepot, 1765–70
Silver
Gift of a descendant, Edward A.
LeRoy, 80.137

The escalating popularity of exotic
beverages—coffee, tea, and chocolate—brought from faraway lands
had a profound and energizing
influence on the forms produced
by silversmiths during the late
seventeenth and early eighteenth
centuries.

Gracie (long-face Jumeau doll),
c. 1882

Bisque head, glass eyes; jointed
wood and composition body
Bequest of Marjorie Phelps Starr,
95.130.1

When a doll named Grace was
given to the Museum of the City of
New York in 1995, it was accompanied by a handwritten invitation to
an 1882 doll's tea party. The text of
the invitation reads: "A Doll's Tea
Party. The compliments of Miss
Mamie Ludington, and of her dollie
Miss Grace, and request the company of yourself and dollie, on Friday,
Dec. 28th to spend the afternoon
and take a social cup of tea. 2 till
5:30. R.S.V.P. 44 East 69th St."

Maker unknown

Handmade paper dolls, 1858
Toy Collection archive

A set of homemade paper dolls,
splendid examples of nineteenth-
century folk art, represents some of
the illustrious guests at the wedding
of the Princess Royal, Queen Victoria's eldest daughter, in 1858.
Shown here are Lady Bessborough
and the Marchioness of Clanri-
carde. Their finery is based on
detailed descriptions in the *London
Court Circular* reprinted in the *New
York Daily Tribune*. Clippings from
the Manhattan newspaper accompanied the paper dolls when they were
donated to the Museum of the City
of New York.

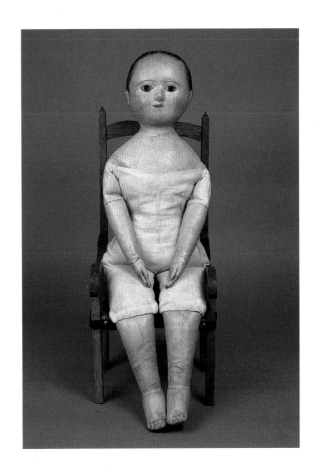

Maker unknown

Mehitabel Hodges ("the Salem Doll"), eighteenth century
Wooden head, body, and arms, with glass eyes; silk gown; lace and ribbon cap
Gift of Mrs. Sophia L. McDonald, 63.46.1

One of the oldest dolls in the United States, Mehitabel was brought to America from Europe in 1724 by Gamaliel Hodges, a sea captain from Salem, Massachusetts, as a gift for his daughter Anstiss. Mehitabel was handed down through seven generations of Hodges' descendants before making the Museum of the City of New York her home.

Izannah Walker (1817–1888)

Cloth doll, c. 1870
Cloth, glue, and stockinette head; sateen body
Gift of Mrs. George B. Agnew, 46.370.12

Izannah Walker would have been considered remarkable in any age. A skilled carpenter, a breeder of canaries, a dabbler in real estate, and a repairer of stoves, she also made dolls, for which she received at least one patent, in 1873. The process by which Izannah created her dolls' heads, presumably perfected over many years, involved pressing layers of glued cloth into molds to form a hard shell, which was then covered with a layer of batting and pasted stockinette. The bodies were made of sateen. Each doll is an individual work of folk art, with its own distinct character. Most of the recognized Izannah Walker dolls are in museums or private collections.

Society in New York

Louis Auchincloss

Society in eighteenth-century New York was, unsurprisingly, dominated by the British governor, the members of his council, and the principal merchants of the town. When the king's representative celebrated a royal birthday at his house in Fort George with a lavish ball, all the notables of the city would forgather to drink the health of the various members of the House of Hanover. As the prosperity of the city waxed, the splendor and luxury of the homes of the local magnates impressed even visitors who knew the stately homes of Britain. But despite all this, society continued to take its cue from London, and its sons were often sent abroad to learn the manners of gentlemen. Newspaper columnists were quick to make fun of this and to mock the affectations and fancy ways of these scions, their quivering minuets and boasted duels, their use of such expressions as "Split me, Madam: by Gad: dam me." And the new emphasis on wealth that seemed part of it all was deplored by the older colonials. Cadwallader Colden complained in 1748: "Tho' the province of New York abounds certainly more in riches than any other of the northern colonies, yet there has been less care to propagate knowledge or learning in it than anywhere else. The only principle of life propagated among the young people is to get money, and men are only esteemed according to what they are worth." Where have we heard that before?

But "the glitter and parade of fashionable life faded out for a time after the Revolution," concludes Esther Singleton in *Social Life under the Georges*, "and what still remained of the extravagance and wild gaiety finally took its departure with the Loyalists." It should be said of that "glitter," however, that it produced an extraordinary consistency of sustained good taste, as is manifested by the myriad photographs in her book of the silver, porcelains, furniture, and clothing from the houses of the Manhattan burghers now collected in various museums.

The society that developed in New York in the first half of the nineteenth century was a considerably staider and soberer affair. The old families who had had the sense to hang on to their real estate—often farmlands in the path of the rapidly growing city—grew rich without having to do very much work, and their husbands and sons were apt to go "downtown" only to collect their rents or, as lawyers, to draw simple wills or trust indentures. In *A Backward Glance*, Edith Wharton described the relaxed lives of her parents and their friends in the aftermath of the Civil War:

A great sense of leisure emanated from their kindly faces and voices. No motors waited to rush them to ball or opera; the opera was just beginning, and 'Opera night' would not have been chosen for one of my mother's big dinners. There being no haste, and a prodigious amount of good food to be disposed of, the guests sat long at table; and when my mother bowed slightly to the lady facing her on my father's right, and flounces and trains floated up the red velvet stair carpet to the white-and-gold drawing room with tufted purple satin arm-chairs and voluminous purple satin curtains festooned with buttercup yellow fringe, the gentlemen settled down again to claret and Madeira, sent duly westward, and followed by coffee and Havana cigars.

But all this was to be considerably stirred up by the arrival of what Edith Wharton called "the invaders," the new industrial rich, the "lords of Pittsburgh," the magnates of oil and rails and coal and steel, who could buy and sell the old families and didn't hesitate to do so. The resistance of the latter was slight; they were not, after all, a landed aristocracy of peers; their basis, like that of their conquerors, was money. Intermarriage was frequent; it was soon hard to tell a Van Rensselaer from a Vanderbilt. All was blurred in a Fifth Avenue that had become a gaudy stretch of Italian palazzos and French chateaux.

For society's gaze was still across the Atlantic to old Europe, and some of the new tycoons—or at least their wives—aspired to join a true aristocracy by marrying their daughters to noblemen or even royalties. Most of these matches were unhappy, for the American girl soon tired of feudal restrictions, but the rage for coronets did not die until the Social Register was full of them.

Henry James in *The American Scene* made the point that one particularly grand dinner party he attended in New York in 1905 seemed to be trying to be something that had no real place or function in a democratic state.

The scene of our feast was a palace and the perfection of setting and service absolute; the ladies, beautiful and gracious and glittering with gems, were in tiaras and a semblance of court trains, a sort of prescribed official magnificence; but it was impossible not to ask oneself with what, in the wide American frame, such great matters might be supposed to consort or to rhyme. The material pitch was so high that it carried with it really no social sequence, no application, and that, as a tribute to the ideal, to the exquisite, it wanted company, support and some sort of consecration. The difficulty, the irony of the hour was that so many of the implications of completeness, that is, of a sustaining social order, were absent.

Another aspect of New York society at its most opulent, in the 1890s and early 1900s, was its lack of interest in arts, or even in the life of the mind. As Mrs. Winthrop Chandler wrote, "The Four Hundred would have fled in a body before a poet, a painter, a musician or a clever Frenchman." In this, it was totally unlike the societies of London and Paris, and caused the emigrations of Henry James and Edith Wharton to those capitals, to name only two of the many American artists so impelled. One of the reasons for this intellectual aridity was the domination of ultrarespectable women who did not begrudge their husbands the long days and nights they devoted to making money so long as the expenditure of it was left to them.

The result was a society where virtue, or at least the rigorous appearance thereof, was more important than the exchange of ideas. Family was the basis of everything, and the daughters, the *jeunes filles à marier*, were not to be shocked by the loose manners of bohemians. Furthermore, whereas in Paris or London an interesting artist could be invited for dinner without his perhaps not presentable spouse—and he would come, too—in New York it was improper not to ask them both, so that if one failed the test, both did. It did not make stimulating dinner parties.

All of this, of course, was changing well before World War I, and the 1920s obliterated it altogether. The society of so-called Wasps, with innumerable exceptions and compromises, continued until World War II to dominate certain institutions: private schools, subscription dances for teenagers, debutante parties, and clubs, but the city's well-to-do had become too numerous and heterogeneous to be rallied under any single group, and the charm of a closed society had largely evaporated. We have witnessed since 1945 the development of a series of societies; it is possible, for example, for a person who has attended a charity ball at the Plaza with hundreds of guests at $500 or $1000 a head, nearly half of whom he knows or knows of, to find himself at an equally expensive party at the Waldorf where he will not know a soul.

It is difficult in 1997 to form any definition of what society is in New York today, though countless newspaper articles are always trying to do so. One can only venture on a handful of generalities. Money, of course, is still the open sesame; that will always be true. Ancestry now counts for nothing; family for little. Looks are far more important than a century ago, when they hardly counted at all. Society today cares very much about appearance and clothes. It likes to make an attractive picture, which is part of the immense role that public relations play in modern life. Accomplishment in almost any field is admired; one hears on all sides people rather smugly claiming, "We are a society of *doers*." But most encouraging of all—or perhaps least discouraging, and regardless of the mixed bag of motives that goes into it— philanthropy dominates the entertainments of society and provides the handiest ladder for the social climber. The ends may not always justify the means, but they certainly help.

NY–Memoryville

Oscar Hijuelos

I am (fortunately or unfortunately) old enough to remember a time when one could find, on most city sidewalks, a certain kind of black wrought-iron, Victorianly splendid streetlamp. The artistry of these lamps, with their plump, petallike ledges was something that always impressed me as a kid, for even then they seemed to harken back to another age of artisanship, one that, to my young imagination, must have flourished hundreds of years before my humble birth in 1951. Great for climbing, those lamps were probably put up on the sidewalks of the Upper West Side of Manhattan around the turn of the century, along with the first tenements, widened streets, and trolley tracks, and have remained among those objects that I cannot separate from my earliest childhood memories of this great "eternal" city. As a matter of fact, my street—118th, off Amsterdam—may have been a blue-collar block, but it was rich with ornament: the heads of Mercury and Zeus sat on elaborate building railings, courtyards were entered though curlicued gates, and neoclassical facades seemed to be everywhere, all beautiful. Much of them are now gone.

In that age of the ornate streetlamps, New Yorkers, in my building at least, actually kept their doors unlocked—as recently as the early 1960s—and no one bothered to put gates up in their windows, though one might look out and see that someone (or someones) had taken the trouble to hang a pair of shoes or trousers on top of one of those aforementioned lamps, that certain kids, known to have a mischievous, if not larcenous side to them, shimmied up to the finial-peak in a display of the skills they'd use in prowling the high ledges of six-story tenement buildings, a kind of dangerous recreation. Kids were always gathered under such lamps, using them for bases in games, until policemen, walking the "beat" or cruising about in green-and-white squad cars chased them away. The kids were tough but essentially moral, the types to have fights and then show up at choir practice. In any event, the only crimes I can remember hearing about involved petty theft and, on one occasion, a stabbing, due to love, but on balance, people felt safe enough. As in a small town, there was a feeling of safety in numbers, to the point that in our park, Morningside, which was on a kind of terraced palisade overlooking the heart of Harlem, things were such that old ladies and young mothers with their strollers and squads of screaming children would sit out on benches, at night, without incident.

I can recall that by day street vendors were common sights: a "scissors man" used to come along pushing a cart with a grinding wheel for sharpening knives, informing the street about his presence by ringing a bell. A man who repaired umbrellas and other household goods soon followed on a bicycle that hauled a small wagon filled with arcane tools. Occasionally one saw a rag man with his cart and horse. Every year we looked forward to the appearances of strolling troubadours, Greeks and Italians I think, playing mandolins, violins, and guitars, pausing before each building as they'd make their way along our street to perform their operatic airs and Neapolitan songs, the tenants throwing coins wrapped in tissue from their windows. People were crazy about sitting out on stoops: there were older kids who sang a cappella rock n'roll songs; there was the prerequisite amount of card playing and joke telling; there were stickball games held in the spring and summer. A game called Three Steps to Germany, which had to do with either the First or the Second World War, was played, as well as, more violently, a punching game called Cow in the Meadow. Occasionally, back in the late 1950s and early 1960s, there were forms of gang warfare waged. Uptown gangs—that is, gangs from above 125th Street—with names like the Sinners and the Assassins would make their way "downtown" to our streets, where the local older kids, Puerto Ricans, Cubans, Irish, Italians, Germans, and African Americans united to make their stand, fights in which, given those pregun days, few people were actually badly hurt.

Situated near Columbia University, on the edge of Harlem, our neighborhood was a place where all nationalities converged. The superintendent in my building was German, the super next door was Irish. Up the street the super was one of my father's best friends, Mr. Martinez, a Mexican who had once been in the merchant marine—that was what had brought him to New York. We had a Japanese restaurant over on the next block, a Japanese food shop on 123rd Street and Amsterdam, across the way from the Manhattan Projects. There was Markowitz's delicatessen on the corner, a few doors down from Columbia University's Casa Italiana, and across the street a 1930s drugstore; there was Adolph's delicatessen and sandwich shop and Freddy's Bodega, a Puerto Rican general store where my mother and father used to buy their plantains and yucca. There was a Jewish furrier with a shop in the neighborhood, and a few doors from that a Cuban beauty salon, where my mother used to hang around with the sisters who ran it; near that, a Puerto Rican liquor store. On Amsterdam, there was a "beatnik" coffee shop with brick floors and leftist political homilies framed on the wall. There was a Jewish-owned candy store around the corner from my Catholic grammar school, Corpus Christi.

The kids I went to school with were about one third Hispanic, one third Irish, one third "others," which pretty much reflected the makeup of the neighborhood. There were college students and professors around, but we "townies," separate, unequal, and distant from the institution looming around us, had little contact with them. Because we were in the vicinity of so many seminaries—on Broadway were the Jewish Theological and Union Theological Seminaries—there seemed to be an abundance of clergy afoot. Every Sunday morning, churches—Riverside, St. John's Cathedral, and my own Corpus Christ—rang their carillon, around eleven. With the bells were the multitude of birds that filled the parks, and it seemed that they sang more loudly on those mornings—perhaps because it was quieter and easier to hear the more subtle things of this life. In any event, there was much tranquillity and music and beauty in the air.

In other parts of Manhattan there were more Hispanic neighborhoods, particularly farther east in Harlem, or down on Amsterdam below 110th, but my father and mother did not seem to mind. They had moved to New York from Cuba in 1943, my father coming north from a farmer's life in Oriente to join several enterprising older sisters, one of whom worked for Pan Am and the other for Macy's department store. The problems their generation encountered, with language, with discrimination, were not as openly discussed as they might be in this age. There were a few Spanish-language newspapers in New York, my father and mother reading *El Diario* along with the *Daily News*, but aside from a few AM radio stations, there wasn't much by way of Spanish-language media around, the way there is today. Mainly, people of their generation focused on financial survival. My father worked in the Biltmore Hotel as a cook in the famous Men's Bar, where he would see the likes of Joe DiMaggio, Ernest Hemingway and, on one occasion, Nikita Khrushchev. His coworkers spoke all kinds of languages, portions of which he had picked up in his years of working with them— French, Italian, German—but his closest friends were Cuban and Puerto Rican, and they used to visit us in our little place, or we would go out to visit them. Dance parties, the rooms crowded with elegantly dressed couples, took place in our first-floor apartment living room, the humble phonograph playing the music of Benny More, Machito, and Tito Puente, among the other fantastic Mambo Kings of that epoch. But if one wanted to go out dancing, there were a lot of places to choose from, West Side dance halls in the eighties and nineties, and more famous mambo palaces, like the Palladium or Park Palace in Manhattan or the Stardust Ballroom in the Bronx. In that period, when men usually wore hats, it was a normal thing for families to get all dressed up and to head out to see friends, *de visita;* to bring presents —pastries and bottles of wine, toys for the kiddies—to listen to music, dance, maybe sing and talk over the events of family life and the world. Cubans, even before the revolution, seemed to be everywhere in the city. I had a godfather, Horacio, who lived down in Chinatown. (My godmother, Carmen, lived upstairs in our building.) We knew a Cuban professor of languages teaching at Columbia, who, nostalgic for Cuba, would come over for dinner and give us kids—myself and my older brother Joe—chocolate bars and a quarter for no particular reason. I had a young and enterprising cousin named Jimmy who lived out in Queens, and whenever he and his wife hosted old-fashioned Cuban meals, the platters of *lechón* and *arroz moros* and fried plantains never stopped coming, all of us heading home sated and exhausted. It seemed that we were always going out, elegant families living all over the city opening their doors to us, their sociability a reenactment of what had taken place back in Cuba, before they had journeyed to New York for whatever reasons—necessity, ambition, want of a change. They were generous, too—it was very much part of the whole idea of "latino-ness," the open door, the gesture of friendship, the soulful admission of unity, amounting to the simple statement that "tú y yo, somos amigos"—you and I, we are friends.

Near Harlem's 125th Street, where we did much of our shopping at stores with names like Annie's and Klein's, one could still find a butcher to freshly kill a hen—if that's what one wanted—or go to the Apollo to hear the Cadillacs or James Brown, and yet a ten-minute subway ride from downtown. I always had the feeling that we lived in the center of New York City. Our influences were many: a fifteen-cent token took us into the heart of Manhattan; museums and the great Central Park; labyrinthian neighborhoods like Chinatown and Little Italy. We didn't have much money, but it seemed that one did not need much money in those days to have a good time. Looking back into "memoryville" I can see what there was about New York that had enchanted people of my mother's and father's generation: there was so much to see and do. I used to accompany my father down to the Biltmore, off Vanderbilt Avenue and Forty-fourth Street, to get his paychecks—and visits into the Biltmore kitchens yielded many good and free meals, especially desserts. We would head out of the hotel and go sightseeing, hang around the Horn & Hardart just to see the setup, look in toy and tobacco shops, walk north to Central Park, and somehow end our journey on 125th Street or at La Marqueta, in East Harlem, with its arcade of stalls, where he would pick up knickknacks, buy fruit and records. Along the way, people always called out to my father by name; even though he was far from his small town in Cuba, I always had the impression that his New York was akin to a series of small pueblos, where he knew people and was treated with respect and affection.

From time to time, it occurs to me that much of that life, along with those antique lamps is gone. My neighborhood, torn up by university expansion, no longer exists; its streets no longer teem with children; most of the old tenements were either torn down or converted into dormitories; the vendors no longer come; and even the railings and much of the stone decorations of the building facades have been removed for safety reasons. I'm probably just as nostalgic for my youth as I am for that old New York, and I am not quite sure what I'm really missing when I pass through this ever-changing city. Things move on, faces change—that's a fact. New York, nevertheless, still enchants me and, I guess, always will.

The Garden Party

Hilton Als

Standing before the intensely feminized dollhouse world that artist Carrie Stettheimer created over a period of nineteen years from 1916 to 1935, leaving it uncompleted, I saw the dimensions of the famous house—29 inches high, two storied, with sixteen rooms—and looked closely at the interiors she had created, each a miniature tribute, really, to the remarkably controlled and reckless sartorial and decorative style championed by her sisters—Florine, a painter, and Ettie, a writer—not to mention their mother, all of them German Jews of great wealth living out their days under the dark eaves of Alwyn Court on West Fifty-eighth Street, and I thought I smelled their feminine selves under the cotton stockings pulled over the legs of one or two dolls in the house, a smell that reminded me of rich women left alone to their own devices, and perhaps old age, when urine splatters against cotton stockings and bed jackets do not protect one against the enduring chill of memory. Looking at the dollhouse, I recalled: the small white comforter draped across her knees had been soaked, the previous winter, in camphor balls and illness. Now the comforter's edge brushed across the tops of her naked feet like a thick veil or shroud, not quite obscuring the clawlike appendages just below the blanket's fringe, mangled monuments to a time when a woman's shoe size could never be too small. She had come of age when petite was synonymous with femininity; now her feet were as deformed as the demands of fashion. Despite—or because of—her misshapen toes, she exercised her interest in accessories by the making and wearing of hats she designed from time to time out of brightly colored fabric—invariably, the fabric she chose to make her hats out of were shot through with gold or silver thread. Often, the shape of those hats complemented, or, rather, emphasized the roundness of her own face, which had in it a mouth whose interior was sometimes coated with a kind of pharmaceutical makeup; the sediment from the pills she took for her various illnesses flecked her tongue and the roof of her mouth like bits of errant face powder.

That mouth, round and opening and shutting like a compact etched not in diamonds but in small white-yellow teeth, issued directives from time to time—to her various children or doctors made bitter through accumulating bodies of illness—but now it did not, as she sat in the discouraged grass turned tea-brown by too little sun and too much shade, her brown feet seeming to grow out of the pinched land she sat in, land cramped by poverty as her feet had once been cramped by cheap shoes. The yard she sat in was not really a yard but a strip of grass bordered on both sides by concrete; the house she lived in with her four teenaged daughters, two younger boys, one yellow-skinned mother, and two or three visiting relatives, contained one television set, a few paperback novels, one or two prints in fauxmahogany frames, all of which was dominated by her potent albeit largely undemonstrative imagination, which her children shared in.

Her imagination was not separate from her unspecified physical calamities, which had come into bloom the winter before, when her feet had not been planted in the not-green grass, and it had not been late summer 1965, and social workers had already begun to come to her home, searching for undeclared food and men, and her son, who sat before her, had yet to conceive of the little theater of play he was performing for her benefit just now —a puppet play with hand-puppets. He had made the puppets himself, just as he had written the play he was speaking, pretending to be two voices waged in moral and physical combat. He performed the play with great ardor as a way of acknowledging the transformative effect her imagination had on him. From her he gleaned that the imagination had intellectual value, and that its value could be used as a way of jettisoning history to the moment. He was performing a puppet play in this moment, but it had grown out of his mother's history. The mother had never built a dollhouse or sculpted a puppet because it never occurred to her that had she done either, it could have made a difference to one or three of her children, let alone herself; that had she built something out of her odd and interesting turn of mind, she might not have turned to disease, which she regarded as a form of creativity: she controlled and shaped her body. Had she built a dollhouse for her girls, her boys, they might not have spent so many years lamenting the loss of things they imagined they once had, but never did.

The boy's soft and colorful puppet heads (the bodies were sticks sheathed in purple and pink silk) grew out of his mother's imaginative style: one of self-decoration and atmospheres replete with theatrics. As a young woman (she was in her early forties now), she had loved dance halls, dancing, and swing bands; her toes had become twisted in her love of those things. Her mangled feet attested to the rigor inherent in making things up—placing affect above cause. At one time, she had wanted the world to believe she had beautiful feet worthy of small shoes. Perhaps the world had.

The mother's imagination, as well as her son's, was substantiated by a similar belief-structure: each recognized mangled feet as such but they did not warrant mention—no one's pain or ugliness did. This was not a form of politeness or social convention—not speaking of the impaired in order to be thought "nice." Rather, mother and son had an interest in recording the gestures and actions made during the present in order to enrich their remembrance of experience, the better to own it, in retrospect. In fact, memory was one of the few things that they could own outright, since, obviously, it had nothing do with purchasing power but invention, which freed them to some extent—especially from the tyranny of her infirmities which, socially, appeared to be separate from herself in that she projected a good and therefore well being. But that was another form of pretending. She and her son had the ability to not be present even as they sat and were polite and smiled at one or another of their interlocutors. This ability made the emotional atmosphere of their menacing home, the awful thick gossip in it, tolerable.

Their ability to be somewhere else also allowed them to ignore the father. In his son's mind, his father was relegated—when he appeared in his imagination not infrequently since he didn't "really" live with the mother—to a dark crawl space beneath the mother's house, as paranoid as he always was, but, perhaps, smaller, loving.

In real life, the father lived with his own mother—a not inappropriate place for him to live since he was a child. When he came to visit, he would huff and puff and eat great steaks; shreds of meat clung to the sides of his greasy baby mouth—his silver hair was greasy, too—because he tried to emulate masculine behavior. The father wanted to be known not as an infant with male genitals that had huffed and puffed in the mother. Always, the father wanted to feel the power he imagined his children's undivided attention would afford him, if only they paid attention to him, which they did when he leveled punishment at them from time to time, not unlike a living, walking and talking doll, trying to burn down the house and the surrounding discouraged green and, along with all that, the mother and son who sat with their mangled feet and hearts racing with dreams, sitting just outside that vengeful doll's jurisdiction, at home in their heads, trying to be something other than themselves. (The Stettheimer Doll House is shown on pages 146 and 147.)

Capturing the Ephemeral

Caroline Rennolds Milbank

Intended to be beautiful or provoking, sober or amusing, simple or sumptuous, fashion is by its very nature fleeting—designed to become obsolete, thereby paving the way for the next novelty (and rung-up sale). Collecting fashion is a way of capturing the ephemeral, pinning down a moment in time. An article of clothing can speak volumes about who designed it, who wore it, and the times in which it was worn. Because everyone wears clothes and has a personal understanding of what they mean, a dress on a mannequin in a museum display can be among the most easily appreciated and understood artifacts from the past.

At its best, fashion holds a mirror to its times, occasionally illuminating a momentous change just as it unfolded. The transmittal across the ocean by wire-service photo of Christian Dior's wantonly luxurious New Look in 1947 was the surest visual sign that the privations of World War II were over. When Rudi Gernreich's topless bathing suit was photographed by *Life* magazine in 1964, the breast-baring yet curiously prudish garment—it was knit of practically Victorian wool—summed up all that was pro and con about the sexual revolution. These were instances in which an item of clothing—more than a book, film, song lyric, or newspaper article—happened to illustrate best what was happening in the world.

That fashion came to be closely allied with change and the quest for the new has to do with its main inspiration—women—and the strides they have made, particularly in the last century. Such elements as the steel stays in a corset, the position of a hemline, feather-light weight of a no-bra bra or the varying heft of a shoulder pad all expose stages in women's development toward (and sometimes away from) modernity.

With the millennium approaching and women's equality more of a fact than a dream, change in fashion has come to be based less on an underlying need and more on an industry-driven appetite for novelty for its own sake. The resulting sense that new styles sometimes seem like the emperor's new clothes is one explanation for the heightened interest in fashions of the past, seen not just in the rise of retro looks but in the increase in the practice of collecting fashion. The fastest-growing area in a sluggish retail industry has been the consignment shop, where collectors purposely seek out two- and three-year-old pieces by favored designers, indicating it is the quality or the look of a design they want, rather than its novelty. Most collectors are in the thrall of older styles and search for them on the Internet, at auctions, swap meets, flea markets, vintage shows, and antique-clothing shops.

The Museum of the City of New York was unusually foresighted seventy-five years ago, when it included articles of clothing in its charter to collect and preserve fine and decorative arts. Although many of the significant first donations were collections of family garments that had been saved for generations, clothing was not something that was being collected in today's sense. In fact, even the most expensive couture creations were still regularly being given away, cut up for doll clothes or cushions, or thrown out on the curb. The Museum of the City of New York was one of the first institutions in the country to recognize that a gentleman's suit or a lady's dress, shown along with furniture, silver, paintings, and other objects in a room setting, helped to flesh out the story of how past lives were led. The tendency today, though, is to treat clothes less as part of a story and more as works of art, with historical significance in their own right.

The first deliberately assembled costume collections, those of museums, developed similarly. Most aimed at representing all the major chronological changes in Western fashion going back as far as the seventeenth century, and at accumulating a wide variety of textiles and costumes from cultures not in the mainstream Western tradition. While women's clothes usually predominate, it has been important to document men's and children's clothes as well. Generally, the holdings in museums reflect what was worn by the wealthy, as they were the ones likely to have kept clothes in the family along with a house or property, and to have considered giving their clothes to a museum, as they would a painting. Consequently, what most museums would like to add to their collections are examples of clothes worn off Park Avenue. Work clothes, rarely having been saved, are the scarcest of all, and much sought after.

Most private collectors have tended to focus less on what important figures in a community wore than on the best design. From the 1960s to the 1980s, when the first private fashion collections were being formed, works by the top French, American, British, and Italian couturiers from the nineteenth and twentieth centuries were the most in demand. And collectors hoped to find pieces that represented the best and most original work of these couturiers. As sources for rare couture have dwindled, and as research into other aspects of fashion history has broadened, to this group of most-wanted names have been added those of the better and more innovative ready-to-wear designers. The biggest change in fashion collecting has been at the lower end—appreciation for mass-produced finds is equaling if not exceeding that for pieces with couture labels. Possibly the fastest-growing area of collecting, and one fueled by interest from Japan, is that of vintage denim; the *New York Times* reported that a pair of early Levi jeans recently sold for $25,000 (a sum that could purchase a respectable number of period Balenciagas, Diors, and Chanels).

The question most often asked about private fashion collections is what do collectors do with them? Fashion designers treat their collections as working design archives, sometimes going as far as taking a garment apart in order to have a pattern made. Those who buy to wear treat their finds the way they do any clothes they buy. The most serious collectors manage their holdings like a museum curator, storing everything away from light, dust, and heat in acid-free tissue in acid-free boxes; researching, cataloguing, and possibly photographing each piece so that future handling can be kept to a minimum. Occasionally, an item will be brought out for study or display, perhaps as a loan to an exhibition, but because of the stretching effect of gravity, the amount of time a garment spends on a mannequin must be limited. Lastly, there are collectors who treat articles of costume—especially, accessories—as decorative objects, perhaps featuring as part of their home decor a wall of pocketbooks, a mantel lineup of antique shoes, or a mannequin in a corner dressed in period garb. Ultimately, fashion is just about the most difficult category of collecting: it's so ephemeral that it's still routinely being discarded instead of saved; its fragility makes caring for it complicated; and, when properly stored, it's completely hidden from view.

Whether it's a pair of jeans, faded to a shade of indigo no computer-generated design could duplicate, or a seemingly simple 1925 Chanel frock that is so exquisitely made it could be worn inside out, the greatest appeal of clothes from the past is that they could no longer be made today. Designers try, but a contemporary copy of a Halston fluid matte silk jersey creation somehow looks flimsy next to the cool weight of the original. Looking into a museum case at a wasp-waisted New Look suit, a bustle-backed nineteenth-century dress held out over a wire-cage undergarment, or even a 1960s bare-midriff mini dress with thigh-high boots, it's possible to experience a variety of responses—ranging from relief that it's no longer socially mandatory to be dressed in a single current reigning mode, to regret that clothes have since become so very functional, to wistfulness that there will never again be another floral embroidery that eerily lifelike, or a velvet that dense and soft, or a color that mesmerizing.

How I Became a New Yorker

Elizabeth Barlow Rogers

No other city has attracted so many eager, ambitious postadolescent children from other regions of the country as has New York. I was once one of the multitude of young Americans who leave their hometowns to join the host of foreign immigrants here. Our challenge, if we don't decide to return home after a few heady and possibly troubled years of living away from our first families and old friends, is to face the grand indifference of the metropolis and learn to call *it* home.

The process of adopting, and adapting to, New York started for me during the exceedingly hot summer of 1963. In that long-ago time of first marriage and career search, I was the wife of a summer associate at a Wall Street law firm and the mother of a four-year-old daughter. From our sublet apartment on Riverside Drive, discovered via the law-school bulletin board, we looked out at the green treetops of the park, and, beyond it, glinting like liquid pewter in the hazy hot sunlight, at the great rolling river.

I had enrolled Lisa in a children's play group at Riverside Church, and each weekday, while the air was still fresh and not yet wavy with heat rising from the baking pavements, we boarded the Number 4 bus for the ride twenty blocks north. Sometimes, while she was engaged in her morning activities, I would sit in the cool, empty sanctuary listening to the organist practice. There, my thoughts would hover about the subject of the summer: would we really move to New York permanently? Could I ever call this city *home?*

Home. It is perhaps the most resonant word in the English language, evoking in most of us our deepest desire to possess a place psychologically, to be rooted somewhere, to belong to a piece of land and its community of inhabitants. Although we are a culture of easy mobility and not much prone to reflection upon the spiritual aspects of this process, the emotional price we pay for our translocations is nevertheless real. Most of us come from places we still think of as home. Now it was my turn in some definitive sense to separate myself from mine.

San Antonio had given me a happier-than-average childhood as I roamed freely with other children of the neighborhood in a northern suburb that was densely covered with live-oak trees. My father's construction business prospered as World War II turned the Texas city into a bustling military crossroads. The modest affluence that rewarded his hard work, and my mother's ambition to have a well-educated daughter made it possible for me to attend Wellesley College. During the summer I am describing, I was between academic years at the Yale School of Art and Architecture, where I was to earn a degree in city planning.

In the long, sultry afternoons, holding Lisa by the hand, I began to take possession of the city through its parks. Robert Caro had not yet written *The Power Broker,* so while she swung or seesawed in the playgrounds of Riverside Park, I could only *experience* the legacy of master builder Robert

Moses, not understanding the extent to which his vision had shaped the park and other parts of the city. Nor did I realize that the curving masonry facades of the buildings we saw on the crest of the slope above us were that way because Frederick Law Olmsted abhorred New York's 1811 grid plan and in 1873 had aligned Riverside Drive according to Picturesque principles of landscape design with the existing topography. But I liked looking at that graceful substance of brick and carved stone through the leafy scrim of the treetops in the park. The Soldiers' and Sailors' Monument, which we could see from the window of our apartment, and Grant's Tomb, which loomed before us as Lisa and I climbed off the bus near Riverside Church, provided a further introduction to turn-of-the-century Beaux-Arts architecture in New York.

Some days we would go to Central Park. Lisa loved scrambling about on its glacially polished outcrops of Manhattan schist, and I started to appreciate the beauty of the park's design, noticing how its builders had created numerous scenes that varied from broad meadows to sky-catching lakes to the intricate byways of the wooded Ramble. There were few signs as yet of its impending deterioration. Congressman John Lindsay would not begin his mayoralty for two more years, and the era of happenings, be-ins, mass concerts, and rules relaxation still lay in the future.

Back in New Haven in the fall, I worked toward completing my city-planning degree, with an emphasis upon open-space planning. By the following summer, the important decision to take up residence in New York had been made, and a small apartment on East End Avenue was rented. It did not have a view of the East River, but Carl Schurz Park was only a block away. The Carl Schurz promenade was a pleasant place to take a walk in the evening, and Gracie Mansion provided a lovely historical vignette of northern Manhattan in its earlier incarnation as a settlement of semirural estates.

The sense that you get, from this and other parks, of the city as a geophysical entity, with its estuarial rivers, marshy bays, and huge protected harbor—580 miles of shoreline in all—struck me as something extraordinary. It was not accidental that New York had become a mighty port, and it was sad now to find so much of the waterfront lifeless and forlorn. But at least, with its commerce diminished, it was replete with opportunities for recreation beyond even Robert Moses's dreams. A civic group called the Parks Association, today known as the Parks Council, was advocating the return of disused piers and industrial sites to the Parks Department.

Joining the Parks Association was an important step in my journey toward becoming a New Yorker, and it brought me my first friendship with someone who was a true New Yorker, both by birth and through a personal code of civic responsibility. Her name was Adele Auchincloss. As president of the Parks Association, Adele encouraged me to write position papers on the waterfront and to testify at hearings on behalf of parks at City Hall. An environmentalist before that word gained currency, she also encouraged me in my efforts to publish my new knowledge of the city's natural history as a book, *The Forests and Wetlands of New York City*. Together we worked to save the Staten Island Greenbelt, which was still mapped as a highway corridor, and to turn the Rockaway beaches and Jamaica Bay over to the National Park Service as the country's first *urban* national park, the Gateway National Seashore.

Urban environmentalism had made me interested in the city's ecological patrimony, and exploring its outlying parklands had schooled me in its geology, botany, and native wildlife. Now my career as a "parkie" sent me to the library to learn about Frederick Law Olmsted, the story of his creation of Central Park in collaboration with Calvert Vaux and of their subsequent partnership in building Prospect Park, Eastern and Ocean Parkways, Fort Green Park, and Morningside Park.

In 1975, Adele accepted an appointment as deputy commissioner of parks. By this time, it was becoming apparent how much of the Olmsted heritage was being forsaken in the carnival spirit of the day and through previous years of indifference to his genius as a landscape architect. Alarmed at the severely deteriorated appearance of Central Park as the city's growing fiscal crisis gave its demoralized management further excuse to lower performance, Adele asked Brooke Astor to fund the creation of the Central Park Task Force. With touching faith that the knowledge of the park's history and design I had won through scholarship could be translated into administrative skills, she asked me to run it.

After Adele left the Parks Department to continue her work as a trustee and volunteer with the New York Botanical Garden and the Natural Resources Defense Council, I stayed on in the Parks Department as the director of the Central Park Task Force. My work to "save Central Park" was made possible by a trio of remarkable women. In the vanguard was Brooke Astor, closely followed by Iphigene Sulzberger and Lucy Moses. With their support, I hired Bruce Kelly, the first landscape architect since the beginning of the twentieth century to focus in a systematic way on the gap between the park's historic intent and its current condition. I was also able to run a summer intern program in which high-school students were trained to perform some of the horticultural tasks that city workers no longer did.

In 1978, Ed Koch became mayor, and his first parks commissioner, Gordon Davis, appreciated the efforts that were barely, but tenaciously, under way in Central Park. On February 27, 1979, the *New York Times* ran a front-page story announcing my appointment as the city's first Central Park Administrator. As yet there was no Central Park Conservancy, and the citizen effort that was to be instrumental in reversing the plight of the park was only starting to materialize. But I was beginning to feel that my Texas mother might be right when she told her friends, "Betsy has sunk down her roots in the stony soil of Manhattan and become a real New Yorker."

Over the past eighteen years, my own sense of rootedness was indeed nourished in the thin glacial soil of Central Park. The park has brought me many rewarding moments as a host of New Yorkers, new and old, joined the Central Park Conservancy, and, section by section, we reclaimed Olmsted's and Vaux's vision. The most rewarding task of all was confuting the conventional wisdom that the park north of Ninety-sixth Street was a "wilderness" in more than one sense and its restoration a quixotic goal. In 1983, Lynden Miller accepted my challenge that she leave her painting studio and combine her talents as artist and gardener by bringing back to life the beautiful 1936 Beaux-Arts Conservatory Garden inside the Vanderbilt Gates, at Fifth Avenue and 104th Street opposite the Museum of the City of New York. The success of this project encouraged other donors to support the restoration of the Harlem Mere, the construction of the Charles A. Dana Discovery Center, and other projects that have made the park's north end safe and beautiful once more.

Today I took a walk in Central Park. I saw ruddy ducks, a swan, and some seagulls on the Reservoir. Plump robins have arrived and are looking for insects in the new grass on Cedar Hill. The yellow-flowering dogwood is in bloom, crocuses and daffodils are up, and behind the Metropolitan Museum, where the furry, swollen buds of the magnolias are beginning to release a few purple petals, a pair of lovers kiss. When I think of this contrived morsel of nature nestled in the city and of the great city itself as part of nature, I am happy. Being in Central Park is like being in a dear familiar village in which everyone is native to the place. Living in New York is wonderful. Yes, I am home.

Louisa A. Coleman (1833–1884)

Winter Scene in Brooklyn, 1853
After Francis Guy, 1820
Oil on canvas
Anonymous gift, 53.2

Louisa Ann Coleman's copy of an 1820 painting by artist Francis Guy (1760-1820) shows Front Street in Brooklyn from Main Street (on the left) to Fulton Street (on the right), an area now partially covered by

approaches to the Brooklyn Bridge and a section of the Brooklyn-Queens Expressway. In one of his newspaper articles, Walt Whitman wrote that this view represents "the most important and compact por-

tion of Brooklyn as it stood in 1820. . . . [It] will forever be invaluable as exhibiting the architectural character of the village at that period; and, in some degree for half a century previous." Coleman, a self-taught artist, produced a number of highly competent works.

Brooklyn, most likely named for Breuckelen, a community in the Netherlands south of Amsterdam, was chartered as a settlement by the Dutch West India Company in 1646. Brooklyn remained an independent municipality until its consolidation with the other boroughs of New York City in 1898.

Anthony Imbert (1794–c. 1836)
Erie Canal Celebration, New York,
1825
Oil on canvas
Anonymous gift, 49.415.1

Artist unknown
Manhattan Company Reservoir,
1825
Watercolor
J. Clarence Davies Collection,
29.100.1579

James and Ralph Clews, after an engraving by Samuel Maverick Cobridge, Staffordshire, England; after 1825

Landing of General Lafayette at Castle Garden, New York, August 1824
Transfer-printed earthenware
Gift of Mrs. Harry Horton Benkard, 34.508.2

Depicted here is the grand beginning of New York City's reception at Castle Garden in honor of the Marquis de Lafayette, beloved hero of the American Revolution. During his twelve-month visit to America, in 1824–25, the elderly French general traveled tirelessly and was feted by New York City several times.

Water has always played a significant part in New York's history—never more so than in 1825, the year the Erie Canal was completed. At the official celebration of that engineering feat, New York Governor DeWitt Clinton, shown here aboard the *Seneca Chief*, ceremoniously poured a keg of Lake Erie water into the Atlantic to symbolize the linking of the Great Lakes with New York Harbor.

Equally beneficial to the economy of New York was the opening of a reservoir by the Manhattan Water Company on Chambers Street that same year. The need for pure water had become ever more urgent as the city grew. Severe epidemics of yellow fever earlier in the century have been attributed in part to an inferior water supply. The Manhattan Water Company, a private concern chartered in 1799, also built an extensive distribution system connecting the Chambers Street reservoir with consumers in different neighborhoods.

Completed in 1842, the Croton Aqueduct was the first conduit to provide a dependable water supply for the city. It was replaced by the larger New Croton Aqueduct in 1890.

Albertus D. O. Browere (1814–1887)

Union Square, 1826
Oil on canvas
J. Clarence Davies Collection,
29.100.1323

The area of New York City known
as Union Square appears on the
New York Commissioner's Plan of
1807 labeled "Union Place." The
word "Union" refers to the junction
of several principal streets and
avenues at that location. The 1807
plan provided for a park there, but
not until 1831 was the promise ful-
filled. This scene shows how sparse-
ly settled were the blocks around
the Bowery and Broadway intersection in 1826. The building boom
that would bring fine residences,
hotels, theaters, and boarding
schools to the square was twenty
years away.

George Harvey (c. 1800–1878)

Nightfall, St. Thomas' Church, Broadway, New York, c. 1837
Watercolor
Bequest of Mrs. J. Insley Blair in memory of Mr. and Mrs. J. Insley Blair, 52.100.11

Artist unknown

Baptising Scene near the White Fort, Hudson River, New York, c. 1834
Watercolor and pastel
J. Clarence Davies Collection, 29.100.2417

Artist unknown

City Hall and Park View, 1835
Oil on copper
Bequest of Mrs. J. Insley Blair, 52.100.15

The liveliness of New York City is reflected in these three images from the mid-1830s. In the twilight view of the neighborhood around St. Thomas' Church, where Broadway meets East and West Houston Streets, the shops are invitingly lit, the lamplighter has begun to make his rounds, and people on horseback mingle with vehicular traffic (including an omnibus bound for Niblo's Garden Theatre). In *City*

Hall and Park View, life pulses around a park that throughout the nineteenth century was the primary gathering place for New Yorkers. The artist who sketched *Baptising Scene* chose to show river traffic on the Hudson, though in 1834 most shipping was still concentrated on the East River. The site is near the foot of Horatio Street, in Greenwich Village. The northernmost Baptist church in the city, North Baptist Church, was located nearby, not far from the White Fort, which is also depicted in the scene.

Nicolino Calyo (1799–1884)

Lemon and Orange Stand, c. 1840
Watercolor
Gift of Mrs. Francis P. Garvan, in
memory of Francis P. Garvan,
55.6.27

Nicolino Calyo (1799–1884)

*The Mead, Ginger and Root Beer
Cart*, c. 1840
Watercolor
Gift of Mrs. Francis P. Garvan, in
memory of Francis P. Garvan,
55.6.7

Among the most charming vignettes of working-class New York
City in the nineteenth century
are the "Street Cries" of Nicolino
Calyo, an Italian artist who arrived
in Manhattan around 1835. Painted
in watercolor with gouache high-
lights, this colorful series of some
fifty images depicts the hustlers and
vendors who hawked their wares on
New York's streets during the 1840s.
Only three original sets are known
to exist.

Lemon and Orange Stand

The Mead, Ginger, and Root-Beer Cart.

E. Didier (active 1843–1871)

Auction in Chatham Square, 1843
Oil on canvas
Anonymous gift, 51.222.1

Artist unknown

Thomas D. Rice Performing His "Jump Jim Crow" Routine at the American Theatre, Bowery, New York, November 25, 1833, c. 1833
Oil on canvas
Gift of Carl F. Grieshaber, 32.483ab

In the mid-nineteenth century, the Chatham Square area of New York was a center for popular entertainment. Among the less formal attractions were the spirited open-air auctions of cheap household goods, such as crockery, baskets, and furniture, along busy Chatham Street itself. More formal, indoor entertainment could be found at the American Theatre on the Bowery, where such popular offerings as "Jump Jim Crow" were presented to overflow crowds. "Jump Jim Crow" was the trademark offering of Thomas D. Rice, an itinerant white performer who (legend has it) based his routine on the shuffling dance of an elderly black stablehand. Performing in blackface (burnt-cork makeup), Rice set a fashion for white-performers-only minstrel shows, which lasted until the mid-1850s.

Attributed to Albertus D. O.
Browere (1814–1887)

Fire at the Tombs, c. 1840
Oil on canvas
J. Clarence Davies Collection,
29.100.1308

Attributed to Henry Inman
(1801–1846)

John Carland, c. 1840
Oil on canvas
J. Clarence Davies Collection,
29.100.1300

In the 1840s, New York's fire fighters were volunteers. Their incentives to serve without pay included exemption from the militia and from jury duty upon completion of ten years with the force, as well as a stimulating social life and an opportunity to play a part in city politics. Organized into engine, hose, and ladder companies, each unit was commanded by a foreman. John Carland, shown here in a painting attributed to Henry Inman, was the longtime foreman of Washington Engine Company 40, also known as the White Ghost Company. The members of an engine company not only pulled the fire truck through the cobblestone streets but also operated the apparatus. The engine depicted in *Fire at the Tombs* is a double-brake hand-pumped fire truck that was operated by two groups of men whose vigorous pumping created the necessary pressure to force water from the tank. Steam-powered fire trucks were invented in 1855, but because they eliminated the need for platoons of men to pump the brakes, the city's volunteer firemen used their political connections and were able to delay the introduction of the new apparatus until 1865, at which time horses assumed the chore of pulling the heavy rigs through the streets. The year 1865 also saw the establishment of a paid New York–Brooklyn Metropolitan Fire Department.

B. J. Harrison (active 1844–1856)

Annual Fair of the American Institute at Niblo's Garden, c. 1845
Watercolor
Gift of Mrs. J. Insley Blair, 51.119

The two famous New York entertainment centers depicted here were both victims of fire, a terrible ravager of American cities before the twentieth century. Niblo's Garden, at Broadway and Prince Street, was an open-air facility, to which Irish impresario William Niblo added a saloon, theater, and hotel complex. It was a popular gathering place for New Yorkers in search of fashionable amusement. Reportedly, the polka was introduced there in 1844.

Destroyed by fire in 1846, Niblo's rose from the ashes the following year and continued to offer first-rate entertainment until 1895, when the building was taken over by the retail magnate A. T. Stewart.

W. S. Parkes (active c. 1853–1857)

Crystal Palace, c. 1853
Reverse oil painting on glass backed
by mother-of-pearl
Gift of Mrs. Samuel S. Schwartz,
64.94

An innovatively constructed cast-
iron and glass building on the site
of present-day Bryant Park, the
Crystal Palace was inspired by the
building of the same name that had
drawn crowds of admiring visitors
to the Great Exhibition in London
in 1851. It opened on July 14, 1853,
as part of the Exhibition of the
Industry of All Nations, the first
world's fair in the United States.
After the exhibition closed in November 1854, space in the Crystal
Palace was leased to various organizations for shows and other events.
Although the Crystal Palace was
reputed to be fireproof, flames
roared through the building on
October 5, 1858, and the technologi-
cal marvel was completely destroyed, reportedly within fifteen
minutes.

C. G. Thompson (1809–1888)

Mr. Israel Bear Kursheedt, 1842
Oil on canvas
Bequest of Alphonse H. Kursheedt,
36.343.3

The German-born merchant Israel
Baer Kursheedt was a formidable
Hebrew scholar, considered the premier student of rabbinical lore in
America. He served a term as president of Congregation Shearith
Israel in New York and established
a society to aid Jewish settlements
in Palestine. His wife, Rebekah
Seixas Kursheedt, was born in
Stratford, Connecticut, where her
father, Gershom Mendes Seixas,
the first Jewish minister of religion
in this country, had moved with his
congregation in 1776, after refusing
to conduct services in British-occu-
pied New York. The Kursheedts's
marriage in 1804 represented the
union of the Sephardic and Ash-
kenazic Jewish communities in
America.

C. G. Thompson (1809–1888)

Rebekah Seixas Kursheedt (Mrs.
Israel Bear Kursheedt), 1842
Oil on canvas
Bequest of Alphonse H. Kursheedt,
36.343.4

Artist unknown

View of New York from Staten Island, c. 1850
Oil on canvas
J. Clarence Davies Collection, 29.100.1311

Staten Island (originally Staten Eylandt) was named for the States General, the governing body of the Netherlands. The first permanent European settlement on the island was established by a small group of Dutch Walloon and Huguenot families. After the Dutch surrendered New Amsterdam to the English, in 1664, Staten Island became part of the Province of New York. In 1683, it was officially named Richmond County, after the residence and title of James Stuart, who two years later became king of England.

Inaccessible except by private boat or public ferry, the island developed slowly. In 1894, in a nonbinding referendum, Staten Island residents voted four to one for incorporation into Greater New York, and this expression of solidarity with the city was formalized in 1898. By 1905, the ferry and school systems, the police and fire departments, and many other public services were run by New York City. The year 1964 was a watershed for Staten Island: with much fanfare the Verrazano Narrows Bridge connecting the island to Brooklyn was opened to traffic. With greatly improved access to the rest of the city came concerns about development, land use, and the environment. When the Board of Estimate, a powerful financial body in which the five borough presidents shared equal power, was abolished in 1990, Staten Islanders' feelings of resentment toward the city intensified. In November 1990, residents voted overwhelmingly to create a special commission to study the feasibility of seceding from New York City and establishing Staten Island as a separate municipality. Three years later, 65·percent of the borough's voters approved a draft charter for an independent city. The matter then went to the state legislature and the governor for final resolution, which has not yet been taken.

Laban S. Beecher (born c. 1805)

Figurehead of Andrew Jackson from the frigate "Constitution," 1834
Painted wood
Gift of Seawanahaka Corinthian
Yacht Club, M52.11

Andrew Jackson was serving his second term as president of the United States when the noted Boston wood-carver Laban S. Beecher created the figurehead of the popular hero illustrated here. It had not long graced the prow of the U.S. frigate *Constitution* when a determined anti-Jacksonian named Captain Samuel Dewey climbed aboard the ship one night, sawed off the head of the figure, and spirited it away in a canvas bag. The *Constitution*'s captain, Jesse D. Elliott, draped the headless figure in the national flag and sailed to New York, where a new head was carved by the firm of Dodge and Son. The repaired figure remained on the historic ship for more than forty years. Recently, the severed head resurfaced in a private collection on the outskirts of Paris.

Joseph W. Appleton

Model of the ship "Half Moon"
Gift of H. Norton Merriman,
Theodore Roosevelt Pelt, Rodney
W. Williams, L. Gordon
Hammersley, Herbert L. Satterlee,
and the Ship Model Society, M34.63

Captain H. Percy Ashley

*Model of the sailing ferry
"Independent," 1784*
Gift of Captain H. Percy Ashley,
M38.11

James E. Buttersworth (1817–1894)

Yachting in New York Harbor, second half of the nineteenth century
Oil on canvas
Anonymous gift, 51.222.2

Victor Gifford Audubon
(1809–1860)
View of Hudson River, c. 1845
Oil on canvas
Gift of Miss Alice Lawrence, 38.188

Fitz Hugh Lane (1804–1865)

Clipper Ship "Sweepstakes," c. 1853
Oil on canvas
Bequest of Theodore E. Blake,
M50.5

The contribution of the Hudson River to the growth and prosperity of New York City is evident in these three nineteenth-century views. In James E. Buttersworth's oil painting, the majestic wind-powered yachts and clipper ships are seen at their best, in the open waters of the Hudson at New York Harbor. A grand view of the Palisades at West 155th Street attracted many artists of the period, including Victor Audubon, a son of the naturalist John James Audubon. In the landscape of 1845 illustrated here, Audubon painted a portrait of himself sitting on a rock in the foreground. The marine artist Fitz Hugh Lane captured not only the harbor entrance at the Narrows and the hills of Staten Island but also

the moment in history when the building of clipper ships reached its zenith with models built expressly for speed. These "extreme" clippers briefly plied the waves alongside the steamships that would replace them.

Nicolino Calyo (1799–1884)

*View of New York, Brooklyn, and
the Navy Yard from the Heights near
Williamsburg,* 1835–45
Gouache on paper
Gift of Mrs. Arthur Douglas
Farquhar, 87.41

Attributed to Nicolino Calyo
(1799–1884)

The Richard K. Haight Family, 1848
Gouache on paper
Bequest of Elizabeth Cushing
Iselin, 74.97.2

This tableau set in a family drawing
room includes Richard K. Haight, a
wealthy New York merchant, his
wife Sarah Rogers Haight, a famous
beauty and socialite, and their four
children. The older daughter is
Lydia. Her brother Richard, who is
seated beside his father, was later
lost at sea on his way home from
England. Five-year-old David, in
the foreground, became a doctor.
The name of the youngest child is
not known.

Charles-Honoré Lannuier

Gaming or trictrac table, 1805–15
Mahogany and mahogany veneer
with ivory and lightwood inlays;
original baize fabric
Gift of Mrs. Harry Horton Benkard,
34.400.1ab

Duncan Phyfe (1768–1854)

Pedestal-end sideboard, c. 1825
Mahogany and mahogany veneer
Gift of Mrs. J. Bertram Howell,
70.86ab

Duncan Phyfe (1768–1854)

Cellaret, c. 1825
Mahogany and mahogany veneer
Gift of Glorianna H. Gibbon,
L5674.1

Visitors to New York City in the
early nineteenth century admired
the elegant mahogany sideboards
laden with silver, cut glass, and crystal that held proud place in local
dining rooms. This example of a
pedestal-end sideboard was made in
the shop of well-known Fulton
Street cabinetmaker Duncan Phyfe
for use in his family's residence.
The matching cellaret holds four
wine bottles. Both pieces descended
through the family of Phyfe's
daughter, Eliza Phyfe Vail.

J. H. Belter & Company
(active 1854–1865)

Center table, 1856–61
Laminated rosewood, marble
Gift of Mr. and Mrs. Ernest G.
Vietor in memory of Mrs. Carl
Vietor (née Ernestine Gunther),
38.53.8ab

Tiffany & Company
(active 1837–present)

"Subway" presentation tray, 1904
Sterling silver
Gift of August Belmont, 68.109

Tiffany & Company
(active 1837–present)

Goelet Prize for Sloops, 1889
Sterling silver
Gift of Mrs. C. Oliver Iselin, M39.1.1

Founded in 1837 as a fancy-goods
and stationery store, the firm of
Tiffany & Company became known
throughout the world for its fine
workmanship and innovative design,
thanks to the marketing skill of
Charles L. Tiffany (1812–1902) and
the stylistic acumen and technical
expertise of silversmith John C.
Moore (active 1832–1851).

Tiffany & Company produced
monumental silver to mark civic
milestones. Construction of the
Interborough Rapid Transit (IRT)

subway line began on March 24,
1900. To mark completion of the
first segment of the line, Tiffany &
Company produced a sterling silver
"Subway" tray featuring a portrait
medallion of contractor John B.
Mc Donald, vignettes of construction and subway stations linked by
track and rails, corporate seals on the
handles, and a map of the line
engraved in the center.

John William Hill (1812–1879)

Broadway and Rector Street, c. 1850
Watercolor
Gift of Forsyth Wickes, 38.19

The great promenade and thoroughfare,
as most people know, is Broadway; a wide
and bustling street, which from the Battery
gardens to its opposite termination in a
country road, must be four miles long.
—Charles Dickens, 1842,
American Notes. . . ., London, 1892

Attributed to Nicholas Biddle
Kittell (1822–1894)

*Mr. and Mrs. Charles Henry
Augustus Carter*, 1848
Oil on canvas
Gift of Mrs. Edward C. Moen,
62.234.12

Samuel B. Waugh (1814–1885)

The Bay and Harbor of New York,
c. 1855
Tempera and watercolor on canvas
Gift of Mrs. Robert M. Littlejohn,
33.169.1

By the late 1840s, Bedloe's Island,
New York's traditional landing station for travelers from overseas, had
become too small to accommodate
the growing number of immigrants. In 1855, the need for an
expanded processing facility
prompted the city to convert Castle
Garden on the Battery, visible at
the left of the painting, used until
then as a concert hall and entertainment center, into a new regis-
tration depot. In 1860, 105,123
immigrants disembarked there, of
whom 47,330 were Irish, 37,899
German, and 11,361 English. Some
details of Samuel B. Waugh's
painting reflect the anti-Irish
sentiment aroused by the arrival of
the destitute Famine Irish: for
example, the label "Pat Murfy for
Ameriky" on the trunk at far lower
right and the caricatured Irish farm
boy in a brown frock coat in the
center foreground.

Artist unknown

*Broadway at Ann Street, Barnum
Museum*, 1855
Colored lithograph
Harry T. Peters Collection,
57.300.582

Drawn by J. W. Hill, engraved by
Henry Papprill

Papprill View of New York, 1855
Colored aquatint
Gift of Mrs. Louis J. Hector, 82.116

In this extraordinary view of Manhattan as a rapidly developing
metropolis, church spires stand out
like exclamation marks above the
commercial hustle and bustle.
Quintessential showman P. T.
Barnum's museum, visible at the
extreme left, attracted numerous
visitors to its natural-history exhibits, "freak shows," and other
forms of entertainment. The unknown artist of *Broadway at Ann
Street* chose Barnum's museum
as a backdrop for a comical treat-
ment of traffic congestion in the
burgeoning city.

Artist unknown

*William Cumbel and Eliza Kate
Wilson*, 1860
Oil on canvas
Bequest of Claire L. Wilson, 69.21

Samuel Lovett Waldo (1783–1861)

Harriet Ashton Clarkson Crosby
(Mrs. William Bedlow Crosby),
c. 1820
Oil on canvas
Bequest of Cornelia Livingston Pell,
38.520.2

American Express Train, 1864
Published by Currier & Ives
Hand-colored lithograph
Harry T. Peters Collection,
58.300.103

Frances F. Palmer

*American Country Life: October
Afternoon*, 1855
Published by Currier & Ives
Hand-colored lithograph
Harry T. Peters Collection, 58.300.12

In 1834, Nathaniel Currier, a twenty-
one-year-old lithographer from
Massachusetts, came to New York
City, where he opened a shop on
Nassau Street across from City Hall
and a factory on Spruce Street. In
1857, he formed a partnership with
James Merritt Ives, a self-trained
artist who had been the firm's
bookkeeper for five years and who
was related to the Currier family by
marriage. The partnership was both
spectacularly prolific and highly prof-
itable. By the time the firm closed its
doors in 1907, it had sold millions of
prints in unlimited editions from an
inventory of over seven thousand
titles. Women contributed to the success of Currier & Ives in several ways.
Thrift-conscious middle-class and
lower-class women were the firm's
primary customers, and the colorists
who hand-tinted the prints were
women. Among the most successful
of the staff artists was Frances F.
(Fanny) Palmer, who was employed
at the firm for twenty-five years. A
sample of her four-part series "American Country Life" is pictured here.

William Sidney Mount (1807–1868)

*Adelaide E. Brooks, John E. Brooks,
and George Spencer Brooks as
Children*, 1853
Oil on canvas
Gift of Mrs. Adelaide Brooks Baylis,
44.302.4

This charming portrait by William
Sidney Mount, America's foremost
genre painter of the mid-nineteenth century, captures a hint of
childish playfulness in the Brooks
children, Adelaide, John Edward,
and George Spencer. In 1894, John
Edward became a partner in the
family's men's-clothing business—
Brooks Brothers, established in 1818.

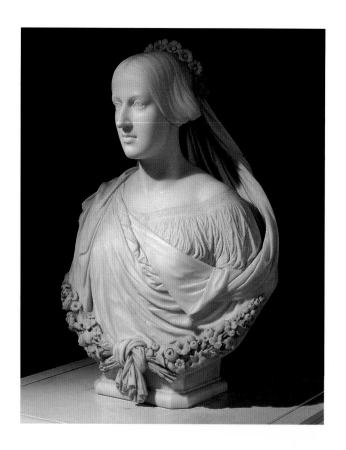

Thomas Crawford (1814–1857)

Louisa Ward Crawford Terry, 1847
Marble
Gift of the Terry Family, 86.173

Portraiture is the most common showcase for a sculptor's talents, and Thomas Crawford's tribute to his wife, Louisa, displays his mastery of the neoclassical style. A notable beauty, Louisa Crawford (1823–1895) was one of the daughters of banker Samuel Ward acclaimed for their beauty as the "Three Graces of Bond Street." Crawford, who worked his way up through the ranks of the New York City stone-cutting firm of Frazee and Launitz, was the first American sculptor to settle in Rome and study his art there. Unfortunately, he died of a brain tumor in his mid-forties.

His wife, who later remarried, willed all the statues and plasters in her late husband's studio in Rome to the City of New York, and the city fathers envisioned a museum in Central Park to house them, but a fire ravaged the studio and all the sculptures were lost.

John Quincy Adams Ward (1830–1910)

August Belmont, Sr., 1891
Bronze
Gift of Morgan Belmont, 53.121

Dean of American sculptors in New York, John Quincy Adams Ward was a great proponent of the so-called Beaux-Arts style, which arose after cognoscenti lost their taste for marble in favor of bronze. Paris and the freer, more naturalistic style developed by Parisian sculptors replaced Rome as a world center for sculpture. Ward's bust of financier August Belmont (1816–1890) is one of the most beautiful in this style.

Belmont was born in Germany and learned banking in the Frankfurt office of the Rothschilds before emigrating to the United States in 1837. He profited from the financial crisis of that year and opened a banking house on Wall Street, where he acted as an agent for the Rothschilds. An active supporter of the Democratic party, he was appointed ambassador to the Netherlands in 1853 by President Franklin Pierce.

Frederick MacMonnies
(1863–1937)

Nathan Hale, 1890
Bronze
Gift of Howard Phipps, 46.289

In the last quarter of the nineteenth century, New York sculptors
began to design spectacular monuments for their city. Frederick Mac-
Monnies' sculpture of Nathan Hale,
the twenty-one-year-old martyr to
American freedom after he was captured by British troops and sen-
tenced to death, is one of the finest.
In this "reduction," or smaller version of the statue, Hale is portrayed
as he concluded his historic speech
with the memorable words, "I only
regret that I have but one life to
lose for my country." MacMonnies,
aware that the statue would grace
City Hall Park, later remarked, "I
wanted to make something that
would set the bootblacks and little
clerks around here thinking, something that would make them want
to be somebody and find life worth
living."

James H. Cafferty (1819–1869) and
Charles G. Rosenberg (1818–1879)

Wall Street, Half Past 2 o'Clock,
October 13, 1857, 1857
Oil on canvas
Gift of the Honorable Irwin
Untermyer, 40.54

On October 13, 1857, a series of events set in motion two months earlier culminated in the suspension of specie payments by all but one of New York's fifty-eight banks, and a financial panic ensued. Banking did not resume in the city until December 12 of that year. The crisis typified one phase of the boom and bust cycles to which Wall Street and the nation's other financial markets were subject—a pattern that continues today.

Several people active in the 1857 crisis are recognizable in the painting: Cornelius Vanderbilt, at the extreme right, arguably the era's most significant manipulator of markets; in the center, Jacob Little, a major figure in the country's mid-nineteenth-century railroad expansion, wearing a light gray drover's topcoat; Frederick Hudson, managing editor of the *New York Herald* and brother of E. W. Hudson, who commissioned this painting, visible next to a bearded man on the left; and the bearded man himself, a self-portrait of the artist James H. Cafferty. As George Borett observed some years after the Panic of 1857 in his *Letters from Canada and the United States,* "Wall Street [is] the New World's 'Hell,' where more fortunes have been made and lost in one year of the last four than in centuries of the lives of other countries."

Johannes E. Oertel (1823–1909)

Woodruff Stables, 1861
Oil on canvas
Gift of Harris Fahnestock, 34.340

The Woodruff Stables on Jerome Avenue in the Bronx had a first-rate reputation among dealers in fine horses. Hiram Woodruff, long acknowledged as the premier trainer of trotters, sold horses to Commodore Vanderbilt, August Belmont (whose wife, Caroline Slidell Perry Belmont, is portrayed at right), Jay Gould, and other connoisseurs at prices as high as $30,000. Jerome Avenue was a boulevard planned to give access to the Jerome Park Racetrack, which opened in 1867.

The Bronx River and the borough of the Bronx, are named for the Swedish immigrant farmer Jonas Bronck, who settled in New Netherland in 1639. The only section of New York City that is part of the North American mainland, the Bronx remained a farming area until 1848, after which immigration and industrialization contributed to its rapid development. By the 1860s, it was generally assumed that the towns on the mainland would be annexed to New York City; and in 1898 the Bronx became one of the five boroughs of New York.

George P. A. Healy (1813–1894)

Caroline Slidell Perry (Mrs. August Belmont, Sr.), 1859
Oil on canvas
Gift of August Belmont IV, 51.317

Caroline Slidell Perry Belmont was a member of America's most distinguished naval family. Her father was Matthew C. Perry, who opened Japan to American commerce in 1853-54; and her uncle was Oliver Hazard Perry, the hero of the battle of Lake Erie. She married banker and diplomat August Belmont in 1849, and the couple soon became known for their elaborate parties, extensive art collection, and passion for horse racing. The Belmonts were among American society's most visible couples during the Gilded Age.

George P. A. Healy, whose elaborate portraits epitomized the grand manner popular at the end of the nineteenth century, was the first American portraitist with an international reputation who had a large and loyal following on both sides of the Atlantic.

R. A. Blakelock (1847–1919)

Fifth Avenue and Eighty-ninth Street in 1868, 1868
Oil on canvas
Gift of Archer M. Huntington, 32.333

George Loring Brown (1814–1889)

Central Park, 1862
Oil on canvas
Gift of Miss Lillian Draper, 72.42

John O'Brien Inman (1828–1896)

Moonlight Skating—Central Park,
The Lake and Terrace, 1878, c. 1878
Oil on canvas
Anonymous gift, 49.415.2

The first landscaped park in the United States, Manhattan's Central Park was created with the advocacy of, for the most part, wealthy merchants and landowners who admired the public grounds of London and Paris and believed such an amenity was the mark of a great metropolis. While the park proved a boon to most New Yorkers, its construction displaced some 1,600 residents and decimated Seneca Village, an African-American and Irish settlement at Eighth Avenue and Eighty-second Street that contained three churches and a school.

Designed by Frederick Law Olmsted and Calvert Vaux, Central Park opened to the public in the winter of 1859.

James R. Van Brunt (1820–1916)

Valley Grove Tavern, Entrance to Port Road, Prospect Park, Brooklyn, 1876
Watercolor
Gift of Mrs. J. Insley Blair, 45.269

Also known as Valley Grove House, the inn seen here was located in the Battle Pass area (the path between two hills) where the battle of Long Island was fought in 1776. Port Road, which intersected the hills dividing Brooklyn from Flatbush, was originally named Valley Grove Road, and the house was named for the road. Valley Grove Tavern was eventually torn down to make way for Prospect Park, which, like Manhattan's Central Park, was designed by Frederick Law Olmsted and

Calvert Vaux. At one point, the designers hoped that the two parks would be connected by a series of wide boulevards. Prospect Park, perhaps the greatest of the urban parks designed by Olmsted and Vaux, remains today the center of Brooklyn's park system.

James Brownlee Simonson

The Back Parlor (Bianchi residence), c. 1875
Oil on canvas
Gift of Mrs. Irving McKesson, 34.74

By 1870, the ongoing uptown migration of New York City's fashionable populace had turned the area from Thirty-second Street to Central Park between Fourth and Sixth Avenues into the city's most desirable residential district. Francisco Bianchi's home stood in the heart of this area, at 61 West Fifty-fifth Street. Bianchi (1833–1899), an importer of artificial flowers and other fancy goods, had moved to Manhattan from Brooklyn. The profusion of sculpture and paintings in his back parlor is in keeping with nineteenth-century notions of the home as a place for nurturing social refinement and interest in the arts.

Howard McClean (1879–1972)

Chinese Theater, c. 1905
Oil on canvas
Robert R. Preato Collection,
91.76.23

John McAuliffe (1848–1921)

Frank Work Driving a Fast Team of Trotters, c. 1891
Oil on canvas
J. Clarence Davies Collection,
29.100.1312

Artist unknown

The Bauern Haus and Carrousel,
c. 1880
Oil on canvas
Gift of Mrs. Bertha Schildt
Hornbostel, 52.323

New Yorkers in search of recreation had a variety of options in the late nineteenth century. Harness racing had become a popular sport by that time; in fact, New York City boasted the first American trotting track and private club for the sport. In the painting by John McAuliffe illustrated here, a favorite trotting strip has taken financier and amateur driver Frank Work past the Watt-Pinckney Mansion at Seventh Avenue and 139th Street.

By 1890, New Yorkers were flocking by the hundreds of thousands to the sandy beaches and seaside amusements on the narrow peninsula that separates Jamaica Bay from the Atlantic. Before the development of railroads, the Rockaways and Coney Island were largely inaccessible except to the wealthy, but in the 1880s a building boom on the western tip of Long Island drove the rich further east to the Hamptons and turned the Rockaways into a lower-middle-class summer refuge. The Bauern Haus hotel was the first seaside pleasure resort built at Rockaway Beach. It was Frederick Schildt, builder and operator of the Bauern Haus, who brought the German carrousel seen in the painting to the grounds of his hotel, and his portrait is part of the gaily painted decoration on the popular "ride."

For stay-at-homes, the city theaters beckoned. In the prosperous decades after the Civil War, many new playhouses were built in Manhattan, and they offered a staggering variety of entertainment. In 1895, a Chinese theater opened at 5-7 Doyers Street—to the delight of Chinese-opera lovers. Part of the thrill of attending performances was the chance that gang warfare, instigated by the tongs, would erupt outside the theater on the streets known then as the Bloody Angle.

Designed by Richard Morris Hunt, executed in Paris by E. S. Oudinot

Leaded glass window, from the home of Henry G. Marquand, 1883–84
Gift of Miss Susan Dwight Bliss, 53.1.29

Worth / Paris

Evening dress, c. 1897
Self-patterned satin and gilt lace
Anonymous gift, 42.146.6ab

Worth / Paris

Fancy-dress costume: "The Spirit of Electricity," 1883
Silk satin, velvet trimmed with gilt metallic bullion
Gift of Countess Laszlo Szechenyi, 51.284.4a-k

Double bracelet-choker necklace combination with three pendant lockets, France, c. 1860
Gold with precious stones
Gift of Henriette A. Laverge, 94.115

Worth/Paris was the couturier of choice for wealthy New Yorkers, who would travel to Paris to acquire sumptuous gowns and fanciful creations to be worn to high-society fetes and costume balls.

Lace parasol with coral handle,
c. 1860
Lace over taffeta cover; ivory and
coral handle
Gift of Mrs. Morgan Belmont,
55.48.1

Fan, c. 1850
Three-color-gold, applied mother-
of-pearl sticks, lithographed mount
Gift of Mary F. Ogden and Charles
W. Ogden, 42.122.7a

*Bedroom from 4 West Fifty-fourth
Street, home of Mr. and Mrs. John
D. Rockefeller, Sr., 1884–1937*
Decorated by George A. Schastey &
Company, 1881
Ebonized woodwork inlaid with
lightwoods; Lincrusta wall covering;
silk damask and velvet hangings
and draperies
Gift of John D. Rockefeller, Jr.,
37.261.1

The Rockefeller bedroom and dress-
ing room installed at the Museum
of the City of New York came from
the residence of John D. Rockefeller, Sr., at 4 West Fifty-fourth
Street. Mrs. Collis P. Huntington,
wife of the railroad magnate, sold
the house with all of its furniture to
Mr. Rockefeller in 1884. Three
years earlier, Mrs. Huntingon (then
Mrs. Arabella Worsham) had en-
larged her residence and employed
the firm of George A. Schastey &
Co. to decorate it in the latest taste.

In 1937, when the building was
slated for demolition following the
death of John D. Rockefeller, Sr.,
John D. Rockefeller, Jr. donated
these rooms to the Museum of the
City of New York and the Moorish
smoking parlor to the Brooklyn
Museum.

Michele Gordigiani (1830–1909)

*Cornelia Ward Hall and Her
Children*, 1880
Oil on canvas
Bequest of Martha Hall Barrett,
61.155

Warren Sheppard (1858–1937)

Brooklyn Bridge Celebration, May 1883, 1883
Oil on canvas
Edward C. Gude, L779

W. Louis Sonntag, Jr. (1869–1898)

The Brooklyn Bridge, c. 1895
Watercolor with tempera
Gift of Mrs. Frederick A. Moore, 54.63

Babylon had her hanging gardens, Egypt her pyramids, Athens her Acropolis, Rome her Athenaeum; so Brooklyn has her bridge.
—Sign hung in a Brooklyn shop window, May 24, 1883

At the time of its construction, the Brooklyn Bridge was the longest suspension bridge in the world, the brainchild of engineer John Augustus Roebling, his wife, Emily, and their son, Washington Roebling. Building the stone and galvanized steel structure took sixteen years, and the project was beset with difficulties. Twenty lives were lost, including that of John Roebling, who was fatally injured when a ferry toppled him from a waterfront piling. Washington Roebling was ren-dered an invalid by "caisson disease" (the bends) and forced thereafter to relay his instructions to workers and managers through his mother. On the day the bridge was opened to the public, May 31, 1883, twelve pedestrians were killed and many more hurt after an anonymous reveler shouted that the bridge was unsafe, setting off a stampede to shore. Since that date, however, the bridge has served New Yorkers well, and the mighty two-towered span has become a city landmark.

James Bard (1815–1897)

"Mary Powell," 1863
Oil on canvas
Gift of Miss Josephine C. Allison,
32.354.1

Self-taught marine painter James
Bard worked with his twin brother,
John Bard (1815–1856), portraying
the steamboats and small sailing
vessels of New York City and the
Hudson River. They left an extensive—and much sought-after—
visual record of New York's
maritime history.

Edward Moran (1829–1901)

Unveiling of the Statue of Liberty,
1886
Oil on canvas
J. Clarence Davies Collection,
34.100.260

On October 28, 1886, a cold and
misty day, the Statue of Liberty was
unveiled on Bedloe's Island in New
York Harbor and dedicated amid
great public celebration. New York
City declared a general holiday,
and Brooklyn closed its schools. As
crowds cheered, horns blared, ships'
bells rang out, and fireworks filled
the air, President Grover Cleveland
formally accepted the gift from
the people of France to the people
of the United States. More than a
century later, the copper statue
of a crowned woman remains the
best-known symbol of freedom in
the world.

August Hepp

Central Park, Gapstow Bridge,
c. 1880
Cyanotype
Print archive

August Hepp

Central Park, Boat House, c. 1880
Cyanotype
Print archive

Peter Baab

View southwest from the roof of
George Ehret's home at Park Avenue
and Ninety-fourth Street, 1882–83
Albumen silver print
Gift of Mrs. Carl Eggers,
print archive

Peter Baab

View northeast from the roof of
George Ehret's home at Park Avenue
and Ninety-fourth Street, 1882–83
Albumen silver print
Gift of Mrs. Carl Eggers,
print archive

In a series of photographs taken in the 1880s, photographer Peter Baab documented the changes that were occurring on the Upper East Side as building lots were leveled and graded and the New York & Harlem Railroad extended its tracks northward to the Harlem River. The coming of the railroad, together with the extension of the Second Avenue elevated train to the Harlem River and the northward progress of the Third Avenue El, made it easy to travel between the eastern sections of Harlem and downtown Manhattan. Waves of Jewish, German, and Italian immigrants, some eager to escape from the overcrowded slum sections of the Lower East Side, and some newly arrived in New York, moved into the hastily constructed uptown tenement buildings and soon transformed East Harlem into an overcrowded workers' community.

Jacob A. Riis (1849–1914) and
Richard Hoe Lawrence (active
1880s)

Hunting River Thieves, c. 1890
Printing-out paper print
Jacob A. Riis Collection, 90.13.1.145

Jacob A. Riis (1849–1914)

*Police Station Lodgers 3, Stranded in
the Strange City*, c. 1890
Printing-out paper print
Jacob A. Riis Collection, 90.13.4.231

Jacob A. Riis (1849–1914)

*Police Station Lodgers 8, A "Scrub"
and Her Bed*, c. 1890
Printing-out paper print
Jacob A. Riis Collection, 90.13.4.236

Born in Ribe, Denmark, in 1849,
Jacob A. Riis arrived in New York in
1870. For a time, he became one of
the thousands of poor immigrants
who sought refuge in police-station
lodging houses, the shelters of last
resort in late-nineteenth-century
New York. By 1887, Riis had found
steady employment as a police
reporter for local newspapers. In
that same year, he began to experiment with flash photography, documenting the horrors of slum
life—both on his own and with the
assistance of other amateur and
professional photographers—and
using his visual evidence to crusade
on behalf of the working poor.

Jacob A. Riis (1849–1914)

Night School in the Seventh Avenue
Lodging House, c. 1890
Printing-out paper print
Jacob A. Riis Collection, 90.13.4.173

Jacob A. Riis (1849–1914) and
Richard Hoe Lawrence
(active 1880s)

*"Black and Tan" Dive in Broome
Street Near Wooster Street.*, c. 1890
Printing-out paper print
Jacob A. Riis Collection, 90.13.4.166

Jacob A. Riis (1849–1914) and
Richard Hoe Lawrence
(active 1880s)

Mullin's Alley, Cherry Hill, c. 1890
Glass lantern slide
Jacob A. Riis Collection, 90.13.2.66

Thomas W. Dewing (1851–1938)

DeLancey Iselin Kane as a Boy, 1887

Oil on canvas

Gift of Miss Georgine Iselin, 40.417

In a work that epitomizes the American Aesthetic Movement, Thomas W. Dewing has placed a realistic rendering of his subject within a flat, highly decorative composition—its flatness emphasized by the large block letters spelling out his subject's name and the vertical palette-knife marks along the lower left margin.

An only child, DeLancey Iselin Kane (1878–1940) had the good fortune to trace his heritage to several grand families. His great-grandfather was the first John Jacob Astor. His father, Colonel DeLancey Astor Kane, is credited with bringing the sport of coaching to America. Eleanora Iselin Kane, his mother, was the eldest daughter of Adrian Iselin, a wealthy New York merchant banker.

Childe Hassam (1859–1935)

Rainy Late Afternoon, Union Square, 1890
Oil on canvas
Gift of Miss Mary Whitney Bangs,
69.121.1

In an 1892 interview, the painter
Childe Hassam described the interest he took in studying urban
crowds and his habit of waiting to
make sketches until "the vehicles
or people disposed themselves in
a manner more conducive to a
good effect for the whole." He
also expressed his delight in
depicting street pavements in
the rain, which he thought "very
pretty when . . . wet and shining,
and caught the reflections of passing people and vehicles." The
artist has turned his interest in
capturing the beauty of sponta-
neous light on wet streets to
create the mood in this painting.

A favored place for large gatherings and mass demonstrations,
Union Square was a place the
Market Florists Association frequently chose to exhibit and sell
flowers—a practice for which formal permission was granted by
the Parks Commissioners in 1891.
That the practice was pursued
informally when Hassam painted
this view may explain why several
clay pots are casually placed on the
rim of the fountain and in the
grass at the lower left corner.

Alexander Cabanel (1823–1889)

Olivia P. Murray Cutting (Mrs. William Bayard Cutting), 1887
Oil on canvas
Gift of daughters and granddaughter of Mrs. William Bayard Cutting, through Mrs. Bayard James, 50.60.1

The Cuttings lived in a town house at 24 East Seventy-second Street, near Madison Avenue, and leased a box at the Metropolitan Opera that is now in the collection of the Museum of the City of New York. Following William Cutting's death in 1912, Mrs. Cutting spent most of her time at their summer residence in Oakdale, Long Island, which subsequently became the Bayard Cutting Arboretum.

Henry Pember Smith (1854–1907)

The Columbian Parade, Washington Square, 1892, 1895
Oil on canvas
Gift of the Rhinelander Real Estate Company, 91.5

The citizens of New York City staged a massive celebration on the occasion of the four-hundredth anniversary of Christopher Columbus's historic voyage of discovery and on October 12 dedicated the Columbus Monument at what has become known as Columbus Circle. The Columbian Parade, held on Monday, October 10, started at Fifty-seventh Street and proceeded downtown on Fifth Avenue to Washington Square.

The Greek Revival house so prominent in this painting of the Columbian Parade was designed in the 1830s by architect Richard Upjohn for William C. Rhinelander. It was one of four Rhinelander family homes along the northwest border of Washington Square, then a haven for New York's affluent patrician families. At the time of the Columbus celebration, the house was occupied by William Rhinelander Stewart, sometimes called "father of the Arch," referring to his role in the replacement of a temporary memorial arch with the permanent marble one that stands today in Washington Square.

L. McKay

Steeplechase Park, Coney Island,
c. 1898–1906
Oil on canvas
Gift of Mrs. George C. Tilyou,
54.167

Coney Island has offered New
Yorkers respite from the city's sweltering heat for almost two centuries.
Its earliest recorded name, Kojin
Eiland, comes from the Dutch for
"rabbit island" and was probably
very descriptive of what was at first
a small isolated settlement. Railroads linking Coney Island to Manhattan were built in the 1870s and
1880s, cutting travel time and cost
dramatically. Huge hotels and
restaurants were constructed to
serve the multitudes who soon came
to enjoy the cool breezes blowing in
from the Narrows and Rockaway
Inlet. Also available were a variety
of less wholesome delights, which

won the resort the nickname
"Sodom by the Sea." Beginning in
1895, canny businessmen like the
developers of Sea Lion Park, began
to build enclosed recreational facilities with elaborate attractions, soon
dubbed "amusement parks." These
parks—Steeplechase, Dreamland,
and Luna Park were the most
famous—provided a respectable
venue where citizens and tourists
might safely enjoy inexpensive pleasures. Steeplechase Park took its
name from the mechanical racecourse installed near the beach.

George Brown Manufacturing Company

Broadway & Fifth Avenue omnibus, c. 1870
Painted tinplate clockwork toy
Gift of Ives Washburn, 39.48a-c

Horse-drawn cars, or "horse railways," began operating in New York City in 1832. The wheels ran on tracks, which reduced friction, allowing the carriages to travel twice as fast as a traditional stage-coach. This improvement in transportation made it convenient for commuters to live as far uptown as Forty-second Street around 1870, when this miniature moving horse car was made.

The toy has a clockwork mechanism designed by George Brown, who founded his company in 1856. It later merged with that of J. E. Stevens to form the American Toy Company.

Louis Marx & Company

Mechanical mouse "Merrymakers" band, 1929
Lithograph tin clockwork toy
Bequest of Cynthia Auerbach, 88.13.2a-e

Louis Marx founded the Marx Toy Company in New York City in 1921, stressing quality at a low price. The company produced every type of toy except dolls, but was best known for its tin windups, such as this jolly musical group. A key is turned to start the mechanism: the piano player bangs the keyboard and the other mice direct, drum, or dance.

Maker unknown

Noah's ark, c. 1850
Painted wooden toy
Gift of Mrs. Douglas M. Moffat, 65.34.1-30b

Among the most popular animal toys of the nineteenth and early twentieth centuries were Noah's arks, commonly referred to as Sunday toys because their biblical theme made them suitable for play on the Sabbath.

Teddy bear

Germany or England, c. 1925
Gift of Paul Ludwig, in memory of
Renée Forsyth, 89.19.1

New York City was the birthplace of
the teddy bear, named in honor of
President Theodore Roosevelt, who
on a famous occasion refused to
engage in the unsportsmanlike
shooting of a bear that had been set
up for him as a target. The first
teddy bear was created by Morris
Michtom, a Russian immigrant
who ran a candy store in Brooklyn
with his wife, Mishka. Inspired by a
cartoon about Teddy Roosevelt's
bear, Michtom created a toy replica
of the bear from brown plush, with
movable limbs and button eyes. He
put it in the front window of his
shop, and by the end of the day he
had sold the prototype and taken
orders for a dozen copies. Concerned
that he did not have permission to
market a toy bearing the president's
name, Michtom wrote to the White
House explaining what he had
done. The president wrote back, "I
don't think my name is likely to be
worth much in the toy bear business, but you are welcome to use it."
Within a year, Michtom had established himself as the Ideal Novelty
and Toy Company, which became
one of the biggest toy manufactur-
ers in America.

Attributed to Benjamin Potter
Crandall

Rocking horse, c. 1850–60
Carved wood
Gift of Leila Burton Luce, in memory of Frank Vincent Burton, Jr.
91.48

This rocking horse is identical to
one attributed to the workshop of
Benjamin Potter Crandall (active
1845–1890) at 49 Cortlandt Street
and 469 Grand Street in New York
City. It belonged to Frank Vincent
Burton, Jr., whose family lived in
Newburgh-on-Hudson and had various properties and residences in
New York City, including the Lord
and Taylor Building and the Burton
Brothers Building on Fifth Avenue.
Frank Burton's daughter said about
her father, "Daddy's lifetime preoc-
cupation was horses—hacking,
hunting, polo, following the races
and attending the sales, so this dear
little rocking horse, which was in
his family's possession, sort of pre-
figured the rest of his life."

Albert Schoenhut Company

Humpty Dumpty circus toys,
c. 1903–28
Jointed wood, elastic

This toy circus of jointed wooden toys, whose parts are strung together with elastic, captures the gaiety and excitement of the big top. Schoenhut's lively figures, exceptional in their clever detailing, were a consistently popular item for some thirty years. Over the decades, the sets expanded from a few pieces to a multitude that included cages, parade wagons, and some sixty painted wooden animals and performers that could be set up in their own ring under a cloth tent.

Fred Pansing (1854–1912)

Sampson and Schley Leading the Fleet into New York Harbor, August 20, 1898, 1898
Oil on canvas
Gift of Dwight Franklin, 31.94.7

When President William McKinley called for 125,000 volunteers to avenge the destruction of the U.S. battleship Maine in Havana Harbor, New York responded with "vigorous" enrollment. The city also held a huge celebration when Admiral William Sampson's American "squadron" arrived fresh from its victory over the Spanish fleet.

Joseph Pennell (1857–1926)

Ferry Wharves, New York, c. 1905
Watercolor
Robert R. Preato Collection, 91.76.39

Joseph Pennell, best known as a printmaker and book illustrator, made fine studies in watercolor, especially of dockside scenes such as this one. The busy harbor evokes the city's energy and booming optimism.

W. Louis Sonntag, Jr. (1869–1898)

Bowery at Night, c. 1895
Watercolor
Gift of Mrs. William B. Miles,
32.275.2

This watercolor depicts the Bowery when wealthy and fashionable residents still strolled through the area, elevated trains steamed above its sidewalks, and streetcars and horse-drawn carriages lined the thoroughfare. This view was also rendered in lithograph form and probably sold for no more than five cents a copy. The artist, W. Louis Sonntag, Jr., had been a child prodigy whose watercolor of the Brooklyn Bridge was exhibited at the National Academy of Design when he was only thirteen years old. Sonntag also died young—at the age of twenty-nine, just three years after he made this painting of the Bowery.

Louis Comfort Tiffany (1848–1933)

Egyptian headdress and collar, 1913
Gift of Julia Tiffany Weld, 75.21.1-2

On February 4, 1913, four hundred
guests attended Louis Tiffany's
Egyptian Fete, an extravagant costume party held at the Tiffany
Studios' New York City showroom,
which had been transformed into
an evocation of the ancient city of
Alexandria at the time of
Cleopatra. In the spirit of the
evening, Tiffany donned the costume of an Egyptian potentate. One
of his daughters wore the headdress
pictured here, which features a
stuffed and mounted baby peacock.

Tiffany Glass and Decorating Company (1892–1900)

"Royal" pattern champagne glasses, c. 1900
Favrile glass
Gift of Mrs. Robert Coleman Taylor, 37.115.3; 37.330

In the early 1870s, Louis Comfort Tiffany began experimenting with glassmaking techniques. In 1885, he formed the Tiffany Glass Company to produce his window designs on a large scale, and by 1894 had perfected the manufacture of "Favrile," a blown glass with an iridescent patina reminiscent of the decomposition of ancient glass.

Tiffany Studios (1900–1932)

Two-part vase, c. 1905
Glass
Gift of Mrs. Carnegie Miller in memory of her mother, Mrs. Andrew Carnegie, 46.351.9ab

Charles Constantin Joseph Hoffbauer (1875–1957)

Roof Garden (Study No. 2 for "Sur les Toits"), 1904
Oil on canvas
Robert R. Preato Collection, 91.76.13

Before the advent of air conditioning, theaters closed down during New York City's hot summers. The first roof garden opened in 1882 atop the Casino Theater and quickly spawned a host of imitations. These alfresco theaters flourished from the early 1880s to the 1920s, when Prohibition and interior cooling systems rendered them obsolete.

Carton Moore-Park (1877–1956)

Washington Square, c. 1914
Oil on canvas
Gift of Howard Moorepark, 76.83

Originally a potter's field and gallows, Washington Square was later reclaimed as a parade ground and then converted to a park. During the second quarter of the nineteenth century Georgian houses lined the park's periphery, several examples of which still stand on Washington Square North. By the early twentieth century, boarding houses appeared on the south side of the park, attracting tenants like the artist-illustrator Carton Moore-Park.

Theresa Bernstein (born 1890)

Bryant Park, c. 1914
Oil on canvas
Robert R. Preato Collection, 91.76.1

Bryant Park was laid out as a potter's field in 1823. The area became a public park in 1847, when it was named Reservoir Square after the adjacent reservoir. The Crystal Palace exhibition hall occupied the site from 1853 until it burned to the ground in 1858. In 1884, the park was given its present name in honor of William Cullen Bryant, the poet and newspaper editor who was also an advocate of public parks. After the main branch of the New York

Public Library rose on the former site of the reservoir in 1899, Bryant Park was redesigned, and in the early years of this century became an active meeting place. During the Depression, it served as a warm-weather "dormitory" for the indigent, and in the 1970s, became a refuge for the homeless and an open market for drug dealers. Subsequent restoration and the opening of an upscale restaurant have restored it to the type of park that Theresa Bernstein painted in 1916.

Samuel H. Gottscho (1874—1971)

Luna Park, Coney Island, 1906
Gelatin silver print
Gift of Gottscho-Schleisner, 54.77.6

Samuel H. Gottscho opened his first professional photographic studio in New York in 1925, after working for many years as an amateur photographer and traveling salesman. In 1936 he and his son-in-law, William H. Schleisner (1913–1962), formed the firm of Gottscho-Schleisner. Together they recorded the commercial and residential architecture of New York City, including interiors and gardens. The meticulous care with which they planned each composition and their unusual

degree of interest in atmosphere and settings elevated architectural photography to a new level of beauty, accuracy, and interest.

Byron Company (active in New York 1888-1942)

Paradise Roof Garden atop Hammerstein's Victoria, 1901-2
Printing-out paper print
Byron Collection, 93.1.1.10852

English photographer Joseph Byron (1847–1923) established his New York studio in 1888. When Joseph was joined by his son Percy (1878–1959), the father-and-son team began what would become five decades of photographic documentation of New York City life. Their work appeared regularly in *Once a Week*, (later *Collier's Weekly*) and other illustrated newspapers, introducing them to a diverse array of future clients. While their commissions had great breadth and their

photographs included a remarkable variety of subjects, Joseph became best known for his prolific work in stage photography and Percy for his documentation of more than 175 ocean liners that docked in New York.

Byron Company (active in New
York 1888–1942)

*Roof Garden, Madison Square
Garden Theatre*, 1899
Printing-out paper print
Byron Collection, 93.1.1.10863

Byron Company (active in New
York 1888–1942)

The New York Herald*'s Four-in-
Hand Drag on Tenth Avenue
between Forty-fourth and Forty-fifth
Streets during the Course of a City
Planning Tour,* 1900
Printing-out paper print
Byron Collection, 93.1.1.18375

Jessie Tarbox Beals (1870–1942)

11 Christopher Street, c. 1910s
Gelatin silver print (modern print
from vintage negative)
Museum purchase, with funds
donated by Lisa and Eric Green,
95.127.18

Arthur D. Chapman (born c. 1890)

Kelly's Alley, 1915
Gelatin silver print
Gift of Arthur D. Chapman,
51.130.11

Between 1916 and 1918, Greenwich
Village burst into the full bloom of
its fame as America's Left Bank.
During this short span of time, a
series of overlapping events and
developments immortalized the
Village as a refuge for those at war
with middle-class manners and
traditions. Arguably the most
expressive—certainly the most
theatrical—incident of the period
was the Arch Rebellion of 1917, as
Village folklore characterizes it.
One frigid winter's night, six con-
spirators, including artists John
Sloan and Marcel Duchamp, broke
into a stairwell at the base of the
Washington Square Arch and
climbed to its summit. Then, in a
blaze of cap-gun fire, they released
balloons and announced that
Greenwich Village was seceding
from the Union and would hence-
forth be known as the Free and
Independent Republic of Washington Square. This mock revolution
symbolized the appropriation of the
Village by many culturally adven-
turous New Yorkers.

Canadian-born photojournalist
Jessie Tarbox Beals, the first woman
press photographer, and photographer Arthur Chapman were both
attracted by scenes in and around
their homes in Greenwich Village
which they rendered in the pictori-
alist style of the period.

Byron Company (active in New
York 1888-1942)

*Chef Leoni Exercising His Cooks
atop the Hotel Commodore,* 1920
Gelatin silver print
Byron Collection, 93.1.1.6074

Byron Company (active in New
York 1888-1942)

Dalton's Swimming Pool, 1922
Gelatin silver print
Byron Collection, 93.1.1.10947

Victor Joseph Gatto (1893-1965)

Triangle Fire (March 25, 1911), 1911
Oil on canvas
Gift of Mrs. Henry L. Moses, 54.75

On the afternoon of March 25, 1911, the top three floors of a ten-story downtown loft occupied by the Triangle Waist Company burst into flames. Unable to escape through exit doors bolted by the management to deter theft, 146 people perished, nearly all female garment workers. The factory owners were tried—and then acquitted, but a great public outcry brought major reforms in the city's building code. An eyewitness to the tragic fire, the artist painted from memory the scene at 22 Washington Place at Greene Street.

Childe Hassam (1859–1935)

Washington's Birthday, Fifth Avenue and Twenty-third Street, 1916
Etching
Gift of Storrs Haynes, 58.333

Grace Ravlin (born 1885)

Red Cross Parade, Fifth Avenue, 1918
Oil on canvas
Gift of the Women's Association of the Brick Presbyterian Church, 56.90

New York's response to historic occasions, truly worthy causes, and shining victories has always been to organize (and enjoy) a large public rally. Patriotism and civic pride prompted the city to sponsor several outstanding parades during World War I. During the Red Cross Parade honoring New York's War Fund Week in May 1918, President Woodrow Wilson unexpectedly joined the ranks of marchers along Fifth Avenue—over 70,000 strong—to emphasize the organization's role as America's second line of defense on the European battlefront. In Grace Ravlin's painting of the Red Cross Parade, the participants have reached the New York Public Library. Also visible in the background is the Knox Building, now Republic National Bank of New York.

Fifth Avenue has long been a favorite route for large parades. The first was organized in 1830 to celebrate the July Revolution in France. Among the greatest parades of the twentieth century was the triumphal ticker-tape procession for astronaut John Glenn on March 1, 1962.

Adrian (1903-1959)

Chorus Girl, 1959
Costume sketch for *Camelot*
(opened December 3, 1960)
Watercolor
Theater archive

Freddy Wittop (born 1921)

Sir (Cyril Ritchard), 1965
Costume sketch for *The Roar of the
Greasepaint—The Smell of the
Crowd*
Gift of Freddy Wittop, 69.93.3

Frances Feist

Louis Armstrong, Cotton Club, 1939
Costume sketch
Gouache, metallic and enamel
pigment on board
Theater archive

Lucinda Ballard (1906–1993)

Blanche (Jessica Tandy), 1947
Costume sketch for *A Streetcar
Named Desire*
Ink and watercolor on
tracing paper
Gift of Lucinda Ballard Dietz,
84.174.2

Ming Cho Lee (born 1930)

Set model for the New York City Opera production of Faust, 1968
Gift of Ming Cho Lee, 69.124.5

Vincente Minnelli (1903-1986)

Jam Session
Set design for "The Show Is On"
Watercolor
Gift of Vincente Minnelli, 77.34.38

William Auerbach-Levy
(1889–1964)

George Gershwin at the Piano, 1926
Oil on canvas
Gift of Max D. Levy, 67.109

George Gershwin (1898–1937),
brought vitality to the Broadway
musical stage during the 1920s
and 1930s. His career as a composer
progressed steadily from revue to
musical comedy to comic opera
to folk opera.

Walter Dean Goldbeck (1882–1925)

*Clifton Webb in Formal Evening
Dress*, 1925
Oil on canvas
Bequest of Clifton Webb, 67.90

Clifton Webb (1893–1966) was born
in Indianapolis and began acting
professionally when he was a boy. By
1911, after brief forays into painting
and opera, he settled on a career in
song and dance. He achieved star-
dom in the late 1920s and early
1930s with such numbers as "I
Guess I'll Change My Plan" (in
The Little Show, 1929) and "Easter
Parade" (in *As Thousands Cheer*,
1933).

Carrie Walter Stettheimer

Stettheimer Doll House, c. 1920
Gift of Miss Ettie Stettheimer,
45.125.1

With her mother and two of her sisters, Carrie Stettheimer presided over New York City's avant-garde between the world wars. The salons held frequently at their home in Alwyn Court on West Fifty-eighth Street attracted the most famous and unorthodox writers and artists of the day. Ettie Stettheimer wrote under the pseudonym Henri Waste, and Florine created fanciful pastel-hued paintings. Carrie proved her own artistic talents in the decoration of her doll house—the art gallery of which was hung with tiny works by the family's artist friends. A miniature *Nude Descending a Staircase* by Marcel Duchamp and an alabaster statue by Gaston Lachaise are among the unique works in the first-floor gallery.

Presented to the Museum of the City of New York in 1945 by Carrie's sister Ettie, the *Stettheimer Doll House* was an immediate favorite with visitors. Since Carrie had originally intended to provide the miniature house with doll inhabitants, in the 1970s the museum staff decorated it as though for a party and peopled it with dolls representing many of the Stettheimers' artistic and literary friends. The small figures, crafted of wire, pipe cleaners, paper, and fabric by John Darcy Noble, are based on the paintings of Florine Stettheimer.

Howard A. Thain (1891–1959)

Opening Night, Ziegfeld Follies,
1926
Oil on canvas
Robert R. Preato Collection,
91.76.15

For a quarter of a century, the popular *Ziegfeld Follies* were an institution on Broadway, delighting the public with sparkling sets, funny lines, catchy tunes, and a chorus of stunningly beautiful girls. Originating with the *Follies* of 1907 at New York's Jardin de Paris, this annual series of musical revues was named after Florenz Ziegfeld, Jr. (1867–1932), its producer. This colorful record depicts the opening night of *No Foolin'*, the 1926 season's *Follies*, at the Globe Theatre (now the Lunt-Fontaine Theatre) on the corner of Broadway and Forty-sixth Street on June 24.

Glenn O. Coleman (1887–1932)

Election Night, 1928
Lithograph
Gift of Mr. and Mrs. A. H. Temple,
58.366

John Sloan (1871–1951)

Snowstorm in the Village, 1925
Etching
Museum purchase, 82.200.2

Frederick Detwiller (1882–1953)

Temples of God and Gold, c. 1923
Oil on canvas
Robert R. Preato Collection, 91.76.17

This view from the eleventh floor
of Carnegie Hall was painted by
Frederick K. Detwiller, a longtime
member and one-time president of
The Artists of Carnegie Hall, Inc.
This organization represented the
painters, sculptors, and graphic
artists who lived and worked in the
famous building on West Fifty-seventh Street. The Artists of Carnegie
Hall also maintained a first-floor
gallery to display members' works.

In *Temples of God and Gold*,
Detwiller captures the monumental
vista from Carnegie Hall—dubbed
a "shrine of the goddess of music"
when it opened in 1891—and glori-
fies New York City's buildings of
commerce and worship.

Peter Hopkins (born 1911)

Riot at Union Square, March 6, 1930,
1947
Oil on canvas
Gift of Peter Hopkins, 66.82

As the Great Depression deepened, Union Square became a gathering place for the jobless. On March 6, 1930, a large rally of unemployed workers and Communist sympathizers was disrupted when police intervened to prevent the crowd from marching to City Hall. The violent confrontation that ensued left more than one hundred demonstrators injured. The public was outraged and eventually won the legal right to assemble in Union Square. The artist, who had observed the contretemps from his studio on the square, painted it from memory some years later.

James W. Kerr (born 1897)

Seventh Avenue Subway, 1931
Oil on panel
Gift of James W. Kerr, 77.16.4

The Broadway-Seventh Avenue subway line starts at South Ferry and travels up through Greenwich Village, the West Side, and Harlem, before ending at 242d Street and Van Cortlandt Park in the Bronx. The mix of passengers featured in this painting attests to the variety of neighborhoods served by the train. Much of the development of the Bronx during the first quarter of the twentieth century was made possible by the northward expansion of this and other lines of the metropolitan transit system.

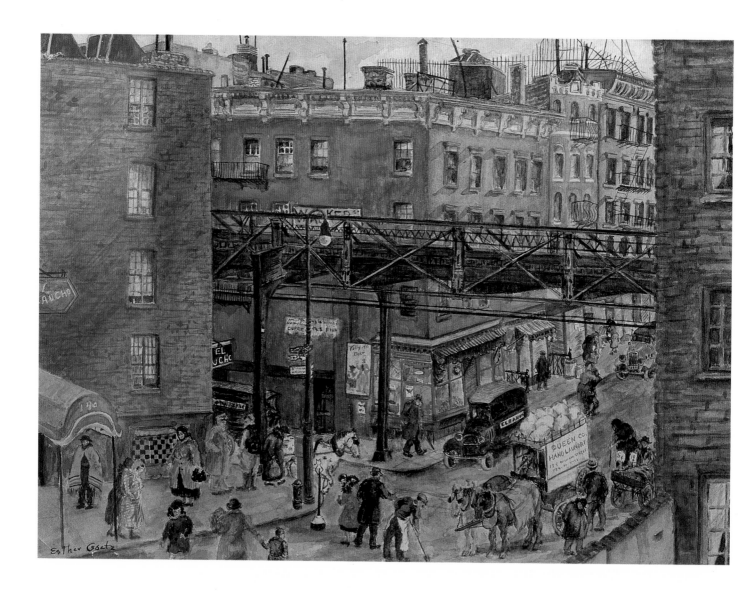

Esther Goetz (1907–1971)

Sullivan Street, 1936
Watercolor
Gift of Mr. George C. McCoy in
memory of his wife Esther Goetz
McCoy, 71.154

This view of Sullivan Street in
lower Manhattan's Little Italy,
where the artist Esther Goetz lived,
registers some of the typical sights
of the district, including its brick
tenements, omnipresent pushcart
vendors, and many different modes
of transportation, ranging from
horse-drawn carts to automobiles
and an elevated railroad.

da Loria Norman (1872–1935)

Holing Through, 1929
Oil on canvas
Gift of Mrs. da Loria Norman,
33.42

Work began on the Independent subway line (IND), the last major addition to the New York City subway system, on March 14, 1925, at St. Nicholas Avenue and 123d Street. This view depicts the satisfying moment when the two teams of "sand hogs" (so named for the soft dirt in which they worked) who had been tunneling toward each other for weeks broke through the wall of earth remaining between them.

As the city became crisscrossed with underground subway lines, the old elevated railroads were torn down. Though we tend to romanticize them today, their noise and dirt, not to mention the shadows they cast on the avenues, caused real-estate values and the quality of life along their routes to decline.

Gottscho-Schleisner, Inc. (active 1925-1960s)

Silhouette, Midtown Manhattan, 1932
Gelatin silver print
Gift of Gottscho-Schleisner, Inc., 34.102.22

Maurice Kish (born 1898)

East River Waterfront, 1932
Oil on canvas
Gift of Maurice Kish, 72.41

Lewis Hine (1874–1940)

Empire State Building Construction,
c. 1930
Gelatin silver print
Empire State Building, L638.5

Lewis Hine (1874–1940)

Empire State Building
Construction, c. 1930
Gelatin silver print
Empire State Building, L638.8

The tallest office tower in the world until 1972, the Empire State Building broke records not only for height but also for speed of construction, in spite of the fact that work began on what is still the most famous skyscraper in the world just weeks before the stock-market crash of 1929. Opening ceremonies were held on May 1, 1931, but leasing proceeded at a snail's pace during the Depression, and for some time quipsters referred to the colossus on Thirty-fourth Street as the Empty State Building.

Rudolph Simmon (1899–1983)

Busy Intersection with Trolley Cars and Elevated Railroad, c. 1927
Gelatin silver print (modern print from vintage negative)
Gift of Mrs. Kay Simmon Blumberg, 94.48.199

Rudolph Simmon (1899-1983)

Group of Boys, c. 1927
Gelatin silver print (modern print from vintage negative)
Gift of Mrs. Kay Simmon Blumberg, 94.48.353

Isac Friedlander

Revival, 1933
Woodcut print
Gift of Mrs. Isac Friedlander,
82.25.1

Don Freeman (1908–1978)

False Alarm, 1934
Lithograph
On permanent deposit from the
Whitney Museum of American Art,
New York, L1226.16

Jacob Kainen (born 1909)

Tenement Fire, c. 1930
Lithograph
Gift of Work Projects
Administration N.Y.C. Art Project,
43.129.20

The more than ten thousand prints
in the collections of the Museum of
the City of New York show many
dimensions of urban life—the
dynamic architectural landscape;
cultural, political, religious, and
sports activities; disasters and celebrations; river and street traffic; and,
above all, human beings of all walks
of life, from the prosperous to the
destitute. The prints illustrated
here, all made in the 1930s, reflect
an interest in experimenting with
new or newly revived printmaking
mediums. The linoleum cut and the
lithograph, as well as the woodcut
and silkscreen, had previously been
used primarily in commercial illustration. Now these techniques were
employed in the pursuit of more
ambitious artistic goals.

Blendon Reed Campbell
(1872–1969)

Queensboro Bridge, c. 1935
Oil on canvas
Gift of Mrs. Alice C. Flenner, 71.121

Originally proposed in 1867 as the Blackwell's Island Bridge (after the strip of land in the East River now called Roosevelt Island), the Queensboro Bridge connecting Long Island City to Manhattan finally opened on March 30, 1909. On that day, it has been said, the borough of Queens entered the twentieth century.

S.S. "NORMANDIE"   GRAND SALON, LOOKING FORWARD   CABIN CLASS.

Byron Company (active in New
York 1888–1942)

*S.S. "Normandie" First Class, Grand
Salon Looking Forward*, 1935
Gelatin silver print
Byron Collection, 93.1.1.11869

The well-established importance of
New York as a port of call for luxury liners continued throughout the
Depression. The French Line passenger ship S.S. *Normandie* went
into service in the Atlantic in the
spring of 1935, arriving in New
York on June 3 after crossing from
Southampton, England, in a record
four days, eleven hours, and forty-
two minutes. The 79,280-ton luxury
liner was 1,029 feet in length overall, and had an 80-foot swimming
pool, twenty-three elevators, and a

dining room modeled after the Hall
of Mirrors at Versailles.

    In January 1942, in the first weeks
of World War II, the United States
impounded the *Normandie* and
renamed her the U.S.S. *Lafayette*.
One month later, the liner was again
docked at a New York City pier,
being converted for troop-transport
service, when she was gutted by fire
and capsized. The cause of the disas-
ter has never been discovered.

Vincent La Gambina (1909–1994)

Life Cafeteria, 1938
Oil on canvas
Gift of the artist, 88.10.1

Since few had money or jobs, the cafeteria became the central meeting place for all sorts of diverse people. For the price of a cup of coffee and a roll, one could sit for hours and hear everything from poetry to politics discussed over the course of an evening.

—Vincent La Gambina

During the difficult Depression years, Vincent La Gambina and other artists sought food and company in Greenwich Village's many inexpensive bohemian canteens. This study of a modestly priced eatery at the corner of Christopher Street and Seventh Avenue, near Sheridan Square, is La Gambina's tribute to the "cafe culture" that sustained many Village artists through the period. Sheridan Square drew tourists, revelers and gawkers hoping to encounter outlandish Village bohemians and local revolutionaries. One contemporary guidebook recommended the Life Cafeteria as a place for sightseers to sit safely "in one section of the room" while watching the "show of eccentrics on the other side."

William Zorach (1887–1966)

Builders of the Future, 1938
Bronze
Gift of Mr. and Mrs. Peter Cardone, 89.12

This boldly stylized bronze sculpture, featuring an interlocked group of workers, builders, and pioneers, was William Zorach's quarter-scale model for an eighteen-foot-high plaster monument that dominated the Rose Court of the 1939 New York World's Fair. The fair, whose theme was "Building the World of Tomorrow," was one attempt to lift New York out of the Great Depression. Built on the ash dumps of Flushing Meadows-Corona Park, in Queens, it went bankrupt in its second year of operation.

Dayton Brandfield

Front Row, 1930
Colored etching
Gift of Work Projects
Administration N.Y.C.
Art Project, 43.129.38

Albert Abramowitz (born 1879)

Wuxtry (Newsboy), 1930
Colored woodcut print
Gift of Work Projects
Administration N.Y.C.
Art Project, 43.129.24

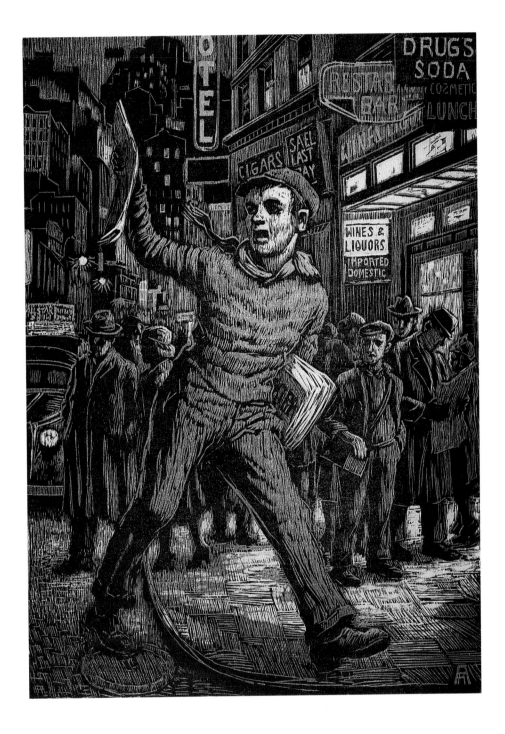

Anthony Velonis (born 1911)

Fulton Fish Market Dock, 1934, 1938
Watercolor on board
Gift of Anthony Velonis, 91.93.5

This watercolor is one of a series
of sketches and paintings commissioned by New York City's Department of Markets for its short-lived
"Fish Tuesday" campaign of 1934.
At the time, New York's fishing
industry was depressed, and the
artist's charge was to stimulate
consumer interest in eating fish.
Sixty years later, in the mid-1990s,
business at the nation's largest
wholesale fish market was again
depressed, but this time the cause
was the violence, extortion, and
fraud on the part of organized
crime that caused seafood suppliers
on the Atlantic and Gulf coasts and
Chesapeake Bay to shun the market
in favor of wholesale distribution
points in other cities.

Lou Barlow

Cafe, 1935
Linoleum cut
Gift of Lou Barlow, 96.83

John J. Soble (born 1893)

Sixth Avenue North from Forty-seventh Street, c. 1936
Oil on canvas
Gift of Mr. John J. Soble, 72.5.1

Toward the end of the Depression, John J. Soble painted this view of tenement rooftops overlooking the soon-to-be-demolished Sixth Avenue El and, in the distance, the glamorous new Radio City Music Hall at Rockefeller Center.

Miklos Suba (1880–1944)

Storefront Mission, Brooklyn, 1943
Oil on canvas
Gift of Susanne Suba, 88.45

This painting of a storefront mission on the corner of Classon Avenue and Dean Street in Brooklyn is part of a series that Hungarian émigré Miklos Suba embarked upon in 1943. Two other notable series of paintings he made in his adopted home of Brooklyn are devoted to barber's poles and cigar-store Indians.

Kay Simmon Blumberg (born 1909)

Berenice Abbott Playing the Concertina, May 1940
Gelatin silver print (modern print from vintage negative)
Gift of Kay Simmon Blumberg, 95.24.4b

Trained as a mathematician, Kay Simmon Blumberg began studying photography under Berenice Abbott at The New School for Social Research in 1939. In 1944, she opened a successful children's portrait studio, but also continued to document New York and other cities.

An Ohio-born artist, Berenice Abbott earned acclaim in Paris during the 1920s as a portrait photographer of the French cultural elite. Returning to the United States in 1929, she was overwhelmed by the growth of New York City and determined to record its future transformation on film. With the enthusiastic support of the Museum of the City of New York and funding from the Works Progress Administration's Federal Art Project, Abbott embarked on her "Changing New York" project. Using the cumbersome 8-by-10-inch view camera favored by architectural photographers, she captured New York's new skyscrapers, highways, and bridges. She was also attracted to its ethnic neighborhoods, decaying waterfronts, and the remnants of rural life still found on Staten Island and in the Bronx. A team of researchers documented the more than three hundred sites Abbott photographed.

Edward Steichen (1879–1973)

Bryant Park Breadline, 1933
Gelatin silver print (by George Tice, 1981–82)
Gift of Sidney Singer, 92.6.2

Shortly after the turn of the century, Edward Steichen became acquainted with Alfred Stieglitz and the Little Galleries of the Photo-Secession, where photography was treated as a fine art. Originally working in an impressionistic, pictorial style, Steichen turned increasingly to documentary photography over the years, working as chief photographer for Condé Nast. After documenting World War II for the United States Navy, Steichen served as Director of Photography at the Museum of Modern Art.

Berenice Abbott (1898–1991)

*Church of God, 25 East 132d Street,
Manhattan*, 1936
Gelatin silver print
Gift of the Metropolitan Museum
of Art, New York, 49.282.42

Berenice Abbott (1898–1991)

Vista from West Street, 1938
Gelatin silver print
Gift of the Metropolitan Museum
of Art, New York, 49.282.79

Berenice Abbott (1898–1991)

Greyhound Bus Terminal, 244–248
West Thirty-Fourth Street and
245–249 West Thirty-Third Street,
Manhattan, 1936
Gelatin silver print
Museum purchase with funds from
the Mrs. Elon Hooker Acquisition
Fund, 40.140.132

Berenice Abbott (1898-1991)

Warehouse, Water and Dock Streets,
Brooklyn, 1936
Gelatin silver print
Museum purchase with funds from
the Mrs. Elon Hooker Acquisition
Fund, 40.140.277

Berenice Abbott (1898–1991)

"El" Second and Third Avenue Lines, Bowery and Division Street, Manhattan, 1936
Gelatin silver print
Museum purchase with funds from the Mrs. Elon Hooker Acquisition Fund, 40.140.67

Berenice Abbott (1898–1991)

Gansevoort Street No. 53, Manhattan, 1936
Gelatin silver print
Gift of the Metropolitan Museum of Art, New York, 49.282.210

Sid Grossman (1913–1955)

Harlem Street Scene, 1939
Gelatin silver print (modern print
from vintage negative)
Gift of the Federal Art Project,
Work Projects Administration,
43.131.9.14

Sid Grossman (1913–1955)

Jitterbugging in Harlem, c. 1939
Gelatin silver print (modern print
from vintage negative)
Gift of the Federal Art Project,
Work Projects Administration,
43.131.9.65

Like Berenice Abbott's "Changing
New York" project, these photographs by Sid Grossman were
made under the aegis of the Works
Progress Administration's Federal
Art Project. The FAP, a relatively
small division of the WPA, was a
relief agency for artists, who were
especially hard hit by the Depression. Its controversial goal was to
show that art, no less than schools
and highways, contributed to the
welfare of all Americans. From its
inception, the FAP (along with sister projects for literature, music, and
the theater) was particularly vul-
nerable to criticism by political con-
servatives, who considered artists to
be lazy slackers, left-wing rabble-
rousers, or both.

Consuelo Kanaga (1894–1978)

Tenement, 1939
Gelatin silver print
Gift of The Citizens' Housing
Council of New York, Incorporated,
39.265.17

Max Yavno (1911–1985)

Big City Playground, 1939
Gelatin silver print
Gift of The Citizens' Housing
Council of New York, Incorporated,
39.265.3

Cecil C. Bell (1906–1970)

Storm over Manhattan, 1938
Oil on canvas
Robert R. Preato Collection,
91.76.21

This painting documents a slice of
Greenwich Village life during the
summer of 1938, when the city
sweltered through a record heat
wave interrupted by sudden and
severe thunderstorms. The view is
from the artist's rooftop at 19 East
Ninth Street.

Jerome Myers (1867–1940)

Street Carrousel, 1936
Oil on canvas
Gift of Mrs. Francis P. Garvan,
76.112

The kaleidoscope of street activity
in New York's immigrant neighborhoods has long been a rich source
for urban genre artists like Jerome
Myers, who focused particularly on
the Lower East Side of Manhattan.

Maurice Kish (born 1898)

The End of an Epoch, 1939
Oil on canvas
Gift of Maurice Kish, 73.35

The earliest form of rapid transit in the United States, the Els, or elevated railways, were threaded through New York City's streets in the last half of the nineteenth century. They quickly became part of city legend, despite complaints that they were noisy and unsightly. With the advent of the subway lines, which were usually built directly beneath the Els, Mayor Fiorello La Guardia began to eliminate the antiquated overhead structures, beginning with the Sixth Avenue line, depicted.

Meyers Rohowsky (1900–1974)

On the Alert at Bryant Park—New York City, 1941
Oil on canvas
Robert R. Preato Collection, 91.76.19

Reginald Marsh (1898–1954)

No. 6–Bowery, 1944
Chinese ink and watercolor
Gift of Mr. Reginald Marsh,
53.107.2

Reginald Marsh (1898–1954)

Harris Theater, New York, 1940
Watercolor and ink
Gift of Mr. Reginald Marsh,
53.107.3

Reginald Marsh was born in Paris
of American parents, both of whom
were artists. The family returned to
the United States when Reginald
was two. Marsh's privileged up-
bringing included private schools,
trips to Europe, and a college education at Yale. A well-known illustrator, painter, and teacher (he
attended New York's Art Students
League and taught there for many
years), he was regarded by many as
the quintessential New Yorker—

in the words of Grace Mayer, first
curator of prints and photographs
at the Museum of the City of
New York, the "unofficial Artist
Laureate" of the city.

James W. Kerr (born 1897)

Times Square Dim-Out, 1944
Oil on canvas
Gift of Mr. James W. Kerr, 77.16.3

Cecil C. Bell (1906-1970)

V-J Day, Times Square (study), 1945
Pastel on board
Anonymous gift, 73.223

Shown here are two images of
Times Square during World War II.
The first documents the unprece-
dented dimming of the Great
White Way (named for its abundance of electric signs); and the second offers a more familiar view of
the midtown hub of the city as a
place of celebration on V-J Day.

Harold Feinstein (born 1931)

Teenagers on Coney Island Beach,
1949
Gelatin silver print
Museum purchase with funds from
the Richard Florsheim Art Fund,
96.121.11

Erika Stone (born 1924)

Ellis Island, c. 1950
Gelatin silver print
Gift of Erika Stone, 96.173.6

Ann Zane Shanks

Date Night: Saturday Night on the Third Avenue El, 1958
Gelatin silver print
Gift of Ann Zane Shanks, 94.32.31

Ruth Orkin (1921–1985)

Man in Rain, 1952
Gelatin silver print
Estate of Ruth Orkin, 96.162

Benn Mitchell (born 1926)

Chinese Hand Laundry, 1952
Gelatin silver print
Gift of Mrs. Esther Mitchell,
95.143.1

Benn Mitchell (born 1926)

Italian Kitchen, 1949
Gelatin silver print
Gift of Mrs. Esther Mitchell,
95.143.14

Rea Irvin (1881–1972)

Window Seat at Christmas, c. 1950
Gouache and charcoal on
illustration board
Gift of Mr. and Mrs. Rea Irvin,
67.100.204

Ernest Fiene (1894-1966)

St. Patrick's Cathedral, 1956
Oil on canvas
Robert R. Preato Collection, 91.76.4

The architectural variety of midtown Manhattan could be called the
subject of this painting. Department
stores, commercial towers, social
clubs, and churches jostle for space
along the streets, and so fast is the
pace of building and demolition in
New York that adjoining buildings
are rarely in the same style. Especially noticeable here is how the
austere rectangle of the Best &
Company storefront contrasts with
the detailed Gothic facade of St.
Patrick's Cathedral.

Anna Goth Werner (1953–1995)

The Crematory (Fresh Pond
Crematory, Ridgewood, Queens),
Oil on canvas, 1978
Gift of Anna Goth Werner, 84.66.6

When a series of ordinances enact-
ed in the 1800s restricted burials in
Manhattan, cemetery developers
bought farmland in rural Queens.
Consequently, that borough today
has a greater concentration of
cemeteries than any other in the
city. Since Queens is also the
nation's most ethnically diverse
county, its memorial parks reflect
the traditions of many vibrant
communities.

Doug Safranek (born 1956)

Still Open, 1994
Egg tempera on panel
Museum purchase, 95.6

This tiny evening view of Greenpoint, a working-class neighborhood in Brooklyn, is dominated by the blazing facade of an all-night minimarket, which has lured a gathering of local patrons. A row of street lamps, occasional windows brightening otherwise dark apartment houses, and the luminous silhouette of distant Manhattan reinforce the notion that the city never sleeps.

Philip Reisman (1904–1992)

Red Wall II, 1978
Oil on canvas
Gift of Mrs. Louise K. Reisman,
80.7

Painted half a century after the
apogee of social realism, Philip
Reisman's depiction of a wall on
Avenue B in Manhattan's East
Village is at once a sober view of
New York City's grittier aspects and
a tribute to the vitality of its inhabitants. Although the built environment predominates, the figures are
not overwhelmed; they are at ease
in their setting.

LEE (Lee George Quiñones)

Howard the Duck, 1989
Oil on canvas
Gift of Martin Wong, 94.114.1

Originating in the 1970s on the walls of subway stations and trains, graffiti spread quickly throughout the city. The artist-writers of the fresh-as-new-paint style were adopted by the galleries, and many began to paint on canvas. *Howard the Duck* first appeared on a Lower East Side playground wall in 1979, and was later replicated on canvas by its creator, LEE.

Eugene O'Neill's New York

Arthur and Barbara Gelb

Eugene O'Neill's world, as anyone familiar with the plays of America's only Nobel Prize dramatist cannot help but be aware, was strewn with ironies.

The house in Danville, California, where he wrote *Long Day's Journey into Night* (and other of the great works of his mature years) was designated after his death a National Historic Site, overseen by the National Park Service. The cottage in New London, Connecticut, where he spent his boyhood summers and which he recreated as the setting for both *Long Day's Journey into Night* and *Ah, Wilderness!,* was carefully restored after being declared a Registered National Landmark by an Act of Congress.

But in New York, with its surfeit of famous native sons, no official notice was ever taken of the fact that O'Neill had been born—on October 16, 1888—in an apartment-hotel called the Barrett House (later renamed the Cadillac). The eight-story building, on the northeast corner of Forty-third Street and Broadway, was demolished in 1940 and replaced by a two-story complex of stores, topped by a towering electric sign advertising Kleenex.

Returning to New York in 1946 after having lived some years in California, O'Neill lamented, "There is only empty air now where I came into this world." It was "a dirty trick," he quipped, to have torn down the hotel where he was born.

To the end of his life, O'Neill remained wistful about the place of his birth. In 1925, for instance, he told an interviewer that every time he passed by the hotel in which he was born, he looked up. "The room was on the fourth floor," he said, "third window from Broadway on the Forty-third Street side. I can remember my father pointing it out to me." In at least one instance, he impetuously hustled a friend up to Room 236, knocked on the door, explained his mission to the startled occupants, and was granted permission to look around.

In 1957, four years after O'Neill's death, the original company of *Long Day's Journey into Night* affixed a plaque commemorating O'Neill's birthplace to the corner shoe store on the site. But when the shop was demolished to make way for an office building in 1972, the plaque was misplaced and later attached to a building on the wrong street corner—a block north of where it correctly belongs. To this day, no one has bothered to move it to its proper site.

While he could joke about the obliteration of his birthplace, O'Neill himself took care to memorialize in *Long Day's Journey into Night* the tragic circumstances of his birth in a New York hotel, an event that shaped him as a man and an artist. Arguably America's most searing tragedy, the play serves as a landmark that will surely outlast any building or plaque. As he revealed in the play, his mother blamed her morphine addiction on his birth—and on the fact that she had been reluctant to conceive him in the first place. "You were born afraid. Because I was so afraid to bring you into the world," the mother in the play confesses to her younger son, Edmund, who represents Eugene.

The Barrett House, with its connotations of personal despair, was but the first in a series of New York apartment-hotels in which Eugene lived with his parents and older brother during his youth. His father was, of course, the matinee idol James O'Neill, whose incessant, coast-to-coast touring during nine or ten months of every year precluded his having any permanent home, apart from his summer cottage in New London; consequently, the O'Neills moved from one Upper West Side hotel to another whenever they were in New York.

In his later years, O'Neill tended to mythologize his summers in New London, declaring it was there that he derived his only sense of home and roots. But it is a fact that—rooted or not—O'Neill did just as much of his growing up in New York as in New London; from his early teens until well into his twenties, he explored the city from its theater district to its gambling dens, from its parks to its red-light district, from its waterfront saloons to the bars and coffeehouses of Greenwich Village bohemia.

It is safe to say that few New Yorkers today are aware of O'Neill landmarks in their midst (some still extant, some—like the Barrett House—built over) that comprised his background and helped form his vision. As residents of the Upper West Side, we ourselves frequently pass by two of the hotels where the O'Neills made their temporary home in the late 1800s and early 1900s. For us, they are still haunted by a ghostly presence: the Belleclaire, on Broadway at Seventy-seventh Street, where Eugene stayed when he was fifteen and on vacations from prep school, and the Lucerne, on Seventy-ninth Street at Columbus Avenue, where we visualize him hovering in the doorway, drunk, after his expulsion from Princeton at the end of his freshman year.

The impact of hotel life on O'Neill's artistic imagination is nowhere more explicitly expressed than in the one-act play *Hughie*, written at the end of his career, just after *Long Day's Journey;* it is set in the lobby of a "small hotel on a West Side street in midtown New York," and through the dialogue of the play's protagonist—a down-on-his-luck gambler—the dreariest aspects of unrelieved hotel living are exposed.

The city's effect on numerous other of O'Neill's works is manifest, even though he has never been regarded as a New York writer. The early sea plays were peopled with the sailors and coal stokers he befriended in a disreputable waterfront saloon-*cum*-rooming house at 235 Fulton Street, known as Jimmy-the-Priest's (demolished in 1966 to accommodate the World Trade Center); one of them, a stoker named Driscoll, became Yank in *The Hairy Ape*, and a barge captain named Christophersen was the model for the father in *"Anna Christie."*

There is a scene set on Fifth Avenue in *The Hairy Ape*, and the saloon in *"Anna Christie"* is modeled on Jimmy-the-Priest's. The same saloon became part of the composite setting O'Neill designated as Harry Hope's, in *The*

Iceman Cometh; Harry Hope's was modeled, as well, on a ramshackle Irish saloon formally called the Golden Swan, but known to its patrons as the Hell Hole. Situated on Sixth Avenue at Fourth Street (and long gone), it was popular with teamsters, gamblers, and gangsters when a handful of aspiring writers and artists discovered it and made it their own.

Roaming the city in his searching and rebellious late teens and early twenties, O'Neill explored the Tenderloin, New York's center of vice (also known as Satan's Circus). It was in this area, stretching from Madison Square to Forty-eighth Street on Manhattan's West Side, that he picked up a first-hand knowledge of the ladies of the night, with whom he later peppered his plays.

The Tenderloin not only contained the red-light district but was the site of gambling dens and illicitly operated saloons, and was headquarters for some of the city's notorious criminals. O'Neill was particularly fond of the Haymarket, on Sixth Avenue, south of Thirtieth Street, a combined restaurant, dance hall, and variety stage, where liquor was served all night long.

Once, in 1911, when O'Neill was living an impoverished and aimless existence, he found five dollars on the sidewalk and headed for Canfield's, a gambling establishment on Forty-fourth Street just east of Sixth Avenue. Within an hour he was $200 ahead—and so drunk that he was evicted. A devoted follower of underworld news, he always relished the fact that he had gambled in a house only a block from where the gangster Herman "Beansy" Rosenthal was murdered six months later.

O'Neill, not surprisingly, also hung about the theater district, where, thanks to a practice known as "professional courtesies," he could identify himself at any box office as James O'Neill's son and, if there were available seats, he would be allowed in. "I don't know if it made me an expert on the drama," he once remarked, "but it made me an awful lot of girl friends."

Years later he still remembered the beautiful legs of a popular musical star named Lotta Faust. "There, my boy, was a love-apple," O'Neill told the critic George Jean Nathan, "and who said anything about acting?" And once, recalling his New York vacations from prep school, he said, "While other boys were shivering themselves into a fit of embarrassment at the mere thought of a show girl, I really was a wise guy."

While he was fond of the gaudy musicals of the era, he was also impressed, at the age of eighteen, by the Moscow Art Theatre's Broadway production of *Hedda Gabler* and—four years later—by Ireland's Abbey Theatre (whose repertory was presented on Broadway in 1911, drawing stormy protest from New York's Irish, offended by the satirical portrayal of their countrymen).

Of *Hedda Gabler,* O'Neill later wrote that he remembered well the impact on him when he "saw an Ibsen play for the first time . . . and then went again and again for ten successive nights." As for the Abbey players, he was greatly struck by "the possibilities of their naturalistic acting." It was seeing them on Broadway for the first time, he said, that gave him "a glimpse" of his "opportunity."

His opportunity came five years later, in 1916, when one of his one-act sea plays, *Bound East for Cardiff* became the first O'Neill drama presented in New York. The Provincetown Players mounted it in the tiny space at 139 MacDougal Street that they initially called the Playwrights Theatre; after moving up the block to Number 133 in 1918, they renamed it The Provincetown Playhouse. One landmark that has been rescued, the playhouse recently renovated by its owner, New York University, with a commitment to revive O'Neill's plays.

The Provincetown Playhouse was the scene in May, 1924, of one of O'Neill's most disputed productions, *All God's Chillun Got Wings*. Set on the Lower East Side, the play centers on the tragic conflict between a struggling black lawyer and his neurotic white wife. It is hard to believe today, but a considerable furor was created when the Provincetowners announced the casting of Paul Robeson as the lawyer. One of the era's most prominent playwrights, Augustus Thomas, publicly commented that the casting was "unnecessary concession to realism," and that by not adhering to the conventions of the day and permitting "a white man to play the part of the negro [sic]," the Provincetowners were embarking on "a tendency to break down the social barriers which are better left untouched."

The city's sensation-minded newspapers predicted that the play would lead to race riots, and the mayor's office—which would have liked to shut down the production but lacked jurisdiction—had to content itself with, at the last minute, withholding the licenses required for the eight child actors (four white and four black) to appear in the first scene; the scene was read from the stage by the director, after he explained to the audience what had happened.

From the beginning of his career, O'Neill startled audiences with his controversial themes and bold use of language. When *Beyond the Horizon* opened in 1920, it astonished the critics, who hailed it as the first native American tragedy ever produced on Broadway. The play heralded a career of innovation that was to stand the conventional—and essentially trivial—Broadway theater on its head.

As with other O'Neill landmarks, the Morosco Theatre on Forty-fifth Street near Broadway, where *Beyond the Horizon* opened, was torn down (in 1982) to make way for the Marriott Marquis Hotel, despite the valiant efforts to save it by a group of prominent theater personalities led by Joseph Papp.

Once O'Neill had begun writing in earnest, he found it distracting to live in New York; he moved away, only returning for productions of his plays. But he maintained an obstinate sentimentality for the Times Square area, treasuring his memories of cobblestoned Broadway, the quiet side streets of the West Forties and the tree-shaded lane a little farther uptown known as the Boulevard. "The green horse cars we used to take when we went to see friends who lived at Seventy-seventh Street had vanished," he once said, dwelling on his lost youth, "and above Fifty-ninth Street the Boulevard had become Broadway."

Always half-humorously resentful of the conspicuous changes he found when he revisited the neighborhood of his birth, he was delighted, in 1948—five years before his death—to receive from an old friend a photograph of the Barrett House as it looked the year he was born there.

"I know of no gift which could have pleased me more," he wrote, thanking his friend and remarking that the figure in the picture leaning against the lamppost outside the hotel obviously "had a bun on."

"I remember seeing him there the day after I was born. You forget there were men in those days and when they decided it was fitting they should go on a drunk, *they went on a drunk!* Not like the weaklings of today, who after ten days of mixed drinks have to have an animal trainer bed them down in Bellevue and gently subdue their menagerie visions! In the old days when I was born, a man—especially one from Kilkenny—went on a five year drunk and finished by licking four cops, and then went home to raise hell because dinner was late."

New York:
American
Architectural
Center

Robert A. M. Stern
with *Thomas Mellins*

A little more than a year ago, on March 10, 1996, the architecture critic of the *New York Times,* Herbert Muschamp, boldly asserted that, "In the last two decades, Los Angeles has eclipsed New York as the country's leading city for contemporary architecture." That sounded very bad for New York, especially because it had been reported in the hometown paper by the hometown critic. True, Los Angeles is home to two or three megasized projects that promise to be very important: the Getty Center, the Disney Hall, and the new Roman Catholic cathedral. But isolated monuments, though they make for hot-spot moments, do not necessarily make for enduring trends. Hot-spot moments often have a way of fizzling as quickly as "high-concept" blockbuster movies on their second weekend. But whether or not L. A. is becoming an architectural center, I do not believe that a fundamental change has occurred in the cultural geography of American architecture as a whole, a geography that has placed New York at the center.

New York is not a hot spot, and it has never been a hot spot. New York is a center. Its architectural fate has never been in the hands of a small group of architects working in a single style. New York's architectural community is nearly as diverse, multifaceted, and composed of independent-minded individuals as is conceivable. There is no "New York style," as there is now said to be a "Los Angeles style." New York has never let itself be pigeonholed by homogenization and categorization.

Many things conspire to ensure New York's position. On the most basic level, there are simply more architects in New York than in any other American city. Not only are there more architects, they are concentrated either in the nation's largest or in its most widely recognized architectural firms. Therefore, at the very least, New York is at the center of the business of American architecture and of American architectural art. In New York, talented young firms elevate apartment remodelings, office interiors, restaurants, and the like into important artistic experiments and high drama. The city is at once a thriving "front office" and "art scene," to be sure, but it is also a "think tank," with a wealth of instructors and institutions to provide the setting for discussion and debate that are so necessary for creative and so sadly absent in most other American cities. Important architectural schools, including Columbia University, Cooper Union, and Pratt Institute, not only train future generations of practitioners but also produce and promote essential scholarship, documentation, and discourse. Professional and civic organizations, such as the Architectural League, the Buell Center at Columbia, the Van Allen Institute, and the Municipal Art Society, also contribute mightily to establishing and maintaining a lively intellectual environment and a vital public discourse. The Museum of the City of New York and the New-York Historical Society consistently hold exhibitions that document the city's evolution in architectural, urban, and cultural terms; equally importantly, the permanent collections and archives of both institutions collectively serve as an invaluable resource for scholars, practicing architects, and the general public, constantly reminding us all that the present and the future are always enriched by a fuller understanding of the past. The contribution of the Museum of Modern Art, which pioneered a department of architecture in 1932, the same year it held its seminal *International Exhibition of Modern Architecture*, should also not be underestimated. From its first years, under the directorship of Philip Johnson, to the present day, the museum has exerted enormous influence, walking a slippery tightrope between scholarship and propaganda.

New York plays another important role in national and international architectural culture by functioning as a hub of architectural book and magazine publishing. New York publishers cover the full range of genres, from books dealing with theory and scholarly research to coffeetable books —from the most abstruse journals to the shelter magazines. The *New York Times*, with a substantial national and international readership, plays a pivotal role in both architectural reporting and criticism. In the 1950s, the *Times* began to take architecture seriously as a subject; in 1963, it appointed Ada Louise Huxtable as the first full-time, staff architecture critic on any American newspaper. Huxtable, as well as her immediate successor, Paul Goldberger, proved to be enormously influential. While the theory-plagued writings of the current architecture critic may not yet have the same impact on the general reader as did those of his predecessors, the *Times* in many ways continues to frame the public debate. Of course, serious architectural journalism is not new to New York: Montgomery Schuyler, an important editor for Manton Marble's *World* and later for the *Times*, was also America's most distinguished architectural critic between the Civil War and World War II, Mariana Griswold Van Rensselaer, who wrote mostly for journals such as *Century Magazine*, was his very close rival. And New York was also home to Lewis Mumford, whose "Sky Line" column in the *New Yorker* between 1931 and 1963 richly documented and brilliantly assessed both the local and national architectural scenes on a regular basis. Today, the *Times* continues in many ways to frame public debate regarding key issues of architecture and urbanism, but a host of other newspapers and magazines also speak out, from the *New Yorker*, to *New York*, to the *New York Observer*.

New York is America's principal crossroads, the essential destination point for visiting architects from around the world; these architects have added, and continue to add, an immeasurable dimension of cosmopolitan luster and variety to what is already a sophisticated and diverse local community. New York's hold upon the imagination of European architects goes back to the 1880s. By the 1920s, the transatlantic appeal of its architecture and urbanism had become almost obsessional. Le Corbusier's 1935 visit to New York, followed by his book, *Quand les cathédrales étaient blanches*, first published in 1937 (but not in English until 1948, as *When the Cathedrals Were White*), established the city as the benchmark against which all modern urbanism and urban architecture was to be measured.

Decades after Le Corbusier's watershed polemic, another book by a European architect affirmed New York's hold on a new generation of Europeans. In *Delirious New York: A Retroactive Manifesto for Manhattan* (1978), the Dutch architect Rem Koolhaas celebrated Manhattan not merely as a prized piece of real estate but as a "laboratory: a mythical island where the invention and testing of a metropolitan lifestyle and its attendant architecture could be pursued as a collective experiment." For beleaguered New Yorkers struggling with quotidian problems of urbanism, Koolhaas's impassioned, celebratory book was a real shot in the arm and proof that, at least in the eyes of some observers, the Big Apple was still not only a vital city but a compelling model of development in which many of the attributes non-New Yorkers dismissed as intolerable were celebrated as the city's strengths.

A front office, an art scene, a think tank, a magnet, and a paradigm, New York is first and foremost an astoundingly complex urban environment. Besides being home to many significant individual examples of virtually every known building type, it has served throughout this century as the premier showplace for the greatest American architectural symbol, the skyscraper. At its best, the skyscraper, a new building type that New York played a pivotal role in shaping, manages to be traditional by taking its place in the continuous web of urban fabric, and totally revolutionary by breaking free as an individualistic, inhabited icon. Although forerunners of the type were built in Chicago, and high-rise office buildings can now be found in cities, suburbs, and adjacent-to-highway sites across the country, it is in New York that the true skyscraper type was first realized and still seems most at home. The tight confines of Manhattan Island are its natural habitat, the setting where the skyscraper most convincingly fulfills its inherent potential. In the post-World War II era, the classic New York skyscraper, with its rugged massing and pinnacled towers, lost favor to a version evolved out of European Modernism. Anonymous, isolated glass-and-steel boxes became the model of excellence. But the intersection of the 1980s' economic boom with a stylistic reevaluation of Modernism conspired to create a renaissance in classic skyscraper shape-making, and once again New York emerged as a leader. Philip Johnson's AT&T Building of 1984 returned the traditional skyscraper type to center stage, creating a symbolically charged corporate monument that picked up where the 1920s towers of New York's skyscraper golden age had left off. Restoring a sense of narrative to the architecture of commerce, AT&T pointed the way toward a renewed appreciation of New York's unique urbanism.

But it is not just isolated, individual buildings that make a great city or define a place as a preeminent urban center. Rather, it is the connective tissue and the ways in which the overall ensemble of buildings are accumulated and shaped that give a city its distinctive character. I believe that Henry James's assertion "a figure is nothing without a setting," which is true of cities in general, is especially true of New York, which at least since the 1920s has celebrated the architectural and urbanistic consequences of density in what has been called a "cult of congestion." Integrally related to the city's physical density and congestion is something less quantifiable but no less palpable: the daily migrations and gatherings of literally millions of people transform New York into a living theater. The most mundane activities—shopping for food, taking a lunch break, going on an evening stroll—all take on the quality of high drama, or, at times, screwball comedy. In architectural and urbanistic terms, this feature of daily life has translated into a sensitivity on the part of architects, planners, and the public alike to the fact that the city is an urban stage. In New York, the significance of public places is as much about what one might call urban entertainment—our restless, democratic, edgy version of town life—as it is about the formal architectural qualities of the places themselves.

In the post–World War II era, New York, like most American cities, lost some of its energy to the suburbs. Most cities suburbanized themselves as if to compete with the car world on its own terms. New York did not. Faced with the "suburban problem," the city has characteristically moved forward by looking to its own past for inspiration. Battery Park City vividly demonstrates how New York's renewed appreciation of its own urban traditions has in recent years pointed the way to a new sense of the possibilities for city building. A ninety-two-acre city-within-a-city built on landfill in the Hudson River alongside the World Trade Center, Battery Park City stands in marked contrast to virtually all postwar schemes for large-scale urban renewal by creating a traditional pattern of streets, continuous walls of buildings, and geometrically defined parks and squares. Although Battery Park City includes apartment buildings designed by such leading practitioners as James Stewart Polshek and Partners, Ulrich Franzen Associates, and Charles Moore, as well as Cesar Pelli's fine restatement of the classic skyscraper type, World Financial Center, containing four towers housing offices for thirty thousand employees, it is the development's urbanistic features and the effective setting they provide for public life—not the individual buildings—that are really important. Pelli's nobly proportioned Winter Garden is a glass-enclosed, temperature-controlled town square realized at metropolitan scale. Outdoors, first-class parks and promenades are successfully embellished with public art by such leading artists as Tom Otterness, Ned Smyth, and Mary Miss. Encircling Battery Park City's public spaces is a staggering array of well-organized and well-publicized cultural events. By appealing thus to the development's working, visiting, and residential populations, Battery Park City reflects high ambitions in societal, as well as strictly architectural terms. As Paul Goldberger argued in a *New York Times* article (May 22, 1988), "the real significance of Battery Park City [is] not the specific designs of its parks or its buildings, good though they are, but [rather] the message this large complex sends about the importance of the public realm."

With a lot of the middle class living and even working in the suburbs, postwar New York declined as an entertainment center. But even that is changing. The rebirth of New York's Forty Second Street-Times Square district is another powerful example of how the city continues to take the lead in creating and implementing daring urban strategies. In song and story, Forty-second Street and Times Square epitomize the concept of edgy urban entertainment. It is a place like no other, with a kaleidoscopically colorful cast of street characters—a place dedicated to make-believe that is very much a part of real life.

Once one of the world's greatest and most famous public places, Forty-second Street and Times Square stumbled after World War II. By the 1980s, plagued with problems relating to drug trafficking and pornography, they seemed doomed to make way for the westward expansion of the midtown office district. But today Forty-second Street and Times Square are being recreated in a new synthesis of offices, theaters, and electronic entertainment that is the object of worldwide attention. This is not an isolated trend of style, but a profound reflection of how, even in a world obsessed with cyberspace gymnastics, urbanistic lessons regarding what makes a public space compelling—indeed, lessons about why we still want to share our experience directly with others—can be learned and relearned. And what better place to learn them than in the most densely populated city in the country, New York?

New York's greatness as an architectural center lies not only in the capacity to creatively build anew and to renew but also to save what is fine from the past. Just as New York has built more than any other city in America in the postwar era, it has also saved more of its past than any other American city. The New York City Landmarks Preservation Commission, established in 1965, two years after the truly tragic loss of McKim, Mead & White's masterful Pennsylvania Station, soon began to change the city's physical aspect profoundly. It also changed the city's power structure, and today the preservationist lobby is probably New York's single greatest force for urban planning. Writing in the *Times* on February 3, 1974, Ada Louise Huxtable noted: "In one decade the cause of preservation has undergone a remarkable transformation from an odd and harmless hobby of little old ladies who liked old houses to an integral, administrative part of city government dealing with an essential part of the city's fabric. From a cultural nicety it has developed into an environmental necessity of important sociological impact—a remarkable consequence no one foresaw."

In numerous ways, New York's pioneering experience with historic preservation has constituted one of the principal success stories of American architecture and urbanism since the 1960s. Nearly eleven hundred individual buildings have been saved from the wrecker's ball, and the very notion of what constitutes a landmark has been both clarified and broadened. At first, the commission tended to make only obvious and uncontroversial choices—opulent buildings designed by well-known architects for wealthy and prestigious clients. But over the course of the last three decades, the commission—and, along with it, the preservation community as a whole—has gained a deep appreciation of the fact that a city's architectural treasure chest is not enriched only by isolated architectural gems, that a city is a complex mélange of the monumental and the vernacular, the fanciful and the utilitarian. Happily, we have developed a preservation philosophy that more effectively evaluates the everyday masterpieces, those more modestly scaled, utilitarian projects, skillfully designed by accomplished, if not always widely recognized, architects that nonetheless play a pivotal role in creating the city's overall texture.

Recently, nationwide attention has been paid to a new and particularly vexing preservation problem: the protection of buildings completed in the recent past, especially those designed in the currently disfavored International Style. In large part the preservation movement grew out of a sense that fine old buildings were being senselessly bulldozed to make way for cheaply constructed, crudely conceived new ones. To a great extent this was true; who can argue that the buildings replacing Penn Station have any merit as public architecture? But the fact remains that many fine and significant buildings in New York have been built in the postwar era and it is our responsibility to preserve them.

A decade and a half ago, it seemed that the idea of preserving Modernist buildings was oxymoronic. Certainly, it was hard to convince preservationists who remembered the destruction of Beaux-Arts Park Avenue to make way for the steel-and-glass corporate buildings of the 1950s that it was time to protect those very buildings. Skidmore, Owings & Merrill's pioneering Lever House of 1952 was designated a landmark in 1982 only after Jacqueline Kennedy Onassis joined the fight. In 1989, Ludwig Mies van der Rohe's and Philip Johnson's Seagram Building of 1958 was designated a landmark in part because the Bronfman family who built it had imposed far stiffer conditions of maintenance and preservation on the building's new owners than even New York's laws call for. Now, the fight to preserve Modernist buildings is beginning to gain momentum. Eero Saarinen's brilliantly conceived TWA Terminal at Kennedy Airport—truly the Grand Central Terminal of the air age—is now protected as the landmark it most clearly is, despite the strongly voiced objections of its owner, the very airline that built it. Currently, the Landmarks Preservation Commission is beginning to consider numerous Modernist buildings for possible landmark designation, and there is even talk of Modernist historic districts on Park and Sixth Avenues—entities the consideration of which would have been inconceivable in the recent past.

Every city experiences ups and downs; New York's vicissitudes are the stuff of legend. Who could forget the famous *Daily News* headline during the fiscal crisis of 1975: "Ford to New York: Drop Dead"? And yet the city recovered—thrived in fact—as a business proposition, as a city bustling with building activity and architectural debate, as the capstone of American urbanism. In our world of instant communication, today's cutting-edge design, be it the invention of someone or some group in Los Angeles or in Timbuktu, is frequently yesterday's news by the time it hits the journals. Perhaps the somewhat jaded—or at least seasoned—perspective of New Yorkers serves to filter out passing fads from genuinely significant trends. I believe that if one wants to see, discuss, and evaluate the best of contemporary American architecture in its fullest variety, and not just sample the flavor of the month, New York remains the place to be, the center of American architecture, the capital of capitals.

Index of Illustrations

Abbott, Berenice, *Church of God, 25 East 132nd Street, Manhattan*, p. 176; *Vista from West Street*, p. 176; *Greyhound Bus Terminal, 244–248 West 34th Street and 245–249 West 33rd Street, Manhattan*, p. 177; *Warehouse, Water and Dock Streets, Brooklyn*, p. 177; *"El" Second and Third Avenue Lines, Bowery and Division Street, Manhattan*, p. 178; *Gansevoort Street No. 53, Manhattan*, p. 179

Abramowitz, Albert, *Wuxtry (Newsboy)*, p. 169

Adelaide E. Brooks, John E. Brooks and George Spencer Brooks as Children, p. 85

Adrian, *Chorus Girl*, p. 142

Albert Schoenhut Company, *Humpty Dumpty circus toys*, p. 123

Alexander Hamilton as an Officer in the Revolutionary Army, p. 21

American Country Life: October Afternoon, p. 84

American Express Train, p. 84

Ames, Ezra, *Catherine Clinton Van Cortlandt* (Mrs. Pierre Van Cortlandt, Jr.), p. 24

Annual Fair of the American Institute at Niblo's Garden, p. 62

Appleton, Joseph W., *Model of the ship "Half Moon,"* p. 69

Ashley, Captain H. Percy, *Model of the sailing ferry "Independent,"* p. 69

Auction in Chatham Square, p. 59

Audubon, Victor Gifford, *View of Hudson River*, p. 70

Auerbach-Levy, William, *George Gershwin at the Piano*, p. 144

August Belmont, Sr., p. 86

Baab, Peter, *View southwest from the roof of George Ehret's home at Park Avenue and Ninety-fourth Street*, p. 108; *View northeast from the roof of George Ehret's home at Park Avenue and Ninety-fourth Street*, p. 109

Back Parlor, The (Bianchi residence), p. 95

Ballard, Lucinda, *Blanche (Jessica Tandy)*, p. 142

Baptising Scene, Near the White Fort, Hudson River, New York, p. 57

Bard, James, *"Mary Powell,"* p. 104

Barlow, Lou, *Cafe*, p. 171

Bauern Haus and Carrousel, The, p. 96

Bay and Harbor of New York, The, p. 78

Bayley, Simon A., *Cake basket*, p. 29

Beals, Jessie Tarbox, *11 Christopher Street*, p. 134

Bedroom from 4 West Fifty-fourth Street, home of Mr. and Mrs. John D. Rockefeller, Sr., p. 99

Beecher, Laban S., *Figurehead of Andrew Jackson from the frigate "Constitution,"* p. 68

Bell, Cecil C., *Storm over Manhattan*, p. 182; *V-J Day, Times Square* (study), p. 189

Belter, J. H. & Company, *Center table*, p. 75

Berenice Abbott Playing Concertina, p. 175

Bernstein, Theresa, *Bryant Park*, p. 129

Big City Playground, p. 181

"Black and Tan" Dive in Broome St. Near Wooster St., p. 113

Blakelock, R. A., *Fifth Avenue and Eighty-ninth Street in 1868*, p. 92

Blanche (Jessica Tandy), p. 142

Blumberg, Kay Simmon, *Berenice Abbott Playing Concertina*, p. 175

Bowery at Night, p. 125

Brandfield, Dayton, *Front Row*, p. 168

Brandywine bowl, p. 26

Broadway & Fifth Avenue omnibus, p. 121

Broadway and Rector Street, pp. 76–77

Broadway at Ann Street, Barnum Museum, p. 80

Brooklyn Bridge Celebration, p. 102

Brooklyn Bridge, The, p. 103

Browere, Albertus D. O., *Union Square*, pp. 54–55; *Fire at the Tombs*, p. 60

Brown, George Loring, *Central Park*, p. 92

Bryant Park, p. 129

Bryant Park Breadline, p. 174

Builders of the Future, p. 166

Busy Intersection with Trolley Cars and Elevated Railroad, p. 160

Buttersworth, James E., *Yachting in New York Harbor*, p. 71

Byron Company, *Paradise Roof Garden atop Hammerstein's Victoria*, p. 131; *Roof Garden, Madison Square Garden Theatre*, p. 132; *The* New York Herald's *four-in-hand drag on Tenth Avenue between Forty-fourth and Forty-fifth Streets during the course of a city planning tour*, p. 133; *Chef Leoni Exercising His Cooks atop the Hotel Commodore*, p. 136; *Dalton's Swimming Pool*, p. 137; *S. S. "Normandie" First Class, Grand Salon Looking Forward*, p. 165

Cabanel, Alexander, *Olivia P. Murray Cutting* (Mrs. William Bayard Cutting), p. 118

Cafe, p. 171

Cafferty, James H., *Wall Street, Half Past 2 o'Clock, October 13, 1857*, p. 89

Cake basket, p. 29

Calyo, Nicolino, *Lemon and Orange Stand*, p. 58; *The Mead, Ginger and Root Beer Cart*, p. 58; *View of New York, Brooklyn and the Navy Yard from the Heights near Williamsburg*, p. 72; *The Richard K. Haight Family*, p. 73

Campbell, Blendon Reed, *Queensboro Bridge*, p. 164

Card table, p. 27

Caroline Slidell Perry, p. 91

Catherine Clinton Van Cortlandt (Mrs. Pierre Van Cortlandt, Jr.), p. 24

Center table, p. 75

Central Park, p. 92

Central Park, Boat House, p. 107

Central Park, Gapstow Bridge, p. 106

Chapman, Arthur D., *Kelly's Alley*, p. 135

Chappel, Alonzo, *Alexander Hamilton as an Officer in the Revolutionary Army*, p. 21 *Chef Leoni Exercising His Cooks atop the Hotel Commodore*, p. 136

Chinese Hand Laundry, p. 194

Chinese Theater, p. 96

Chorus Girl, p. 142

Church of God, 25 East 132nd Street, Manhattan, p. 176

City Hall and Park View, p. 57

Clews, James and Ralph, *Landing of General Lafayette at Castle Garden, New York, August 1824*, p. 53

Clifton Webb in Formal Evening Dress, p. 145

Clipper Ship "Sweepstakes," p. 71

Cloth doll, p. 31

Coffeepot, p. 29

Coleman, Glenn O., *Election Night*, p. 150

Coleman, Louisa A., *Winter Scene in Brooklyn*, pp. 50–51

Columbian Parade, Washington Square, 1892, The, p. 119

Cornelia Ward Hall and Her Children, pp. 100–101

Court suit, p. 22

Crandall, Benjamin Potter, *Rocking horse*, p. 122

Crawford, Thomas, *Louisa Ward Crawford Terry*, p. 86

Crematory, The (Fresh Pond Crematory, Ridgewood, Queens), p. 198

Crystal Palace, p. 63

Currier & Ives, *American Country Life: October Afternoon*, p. 84; *American Express Train*, p. 84

Dalton's Swimming Pool, p. 137

Date Night: Saturday Night on the Third Avenue El, p. 192

DeLancey Iselin Kane as a Boy, p. 115

Detwiller, Frederick, *Temples of God and Gold*, p. 151

Dewing, Thomas W., *DeLancey Iselin Kane as a Boy*, p. 115

Didier, E., *Auction in Chatham Square*, p. 59

Double bracelet-choker necklace combination with three pendant lockets, p. 98

Duyckinck I, Gerardus, *Moses Levy*, p. 18; *Grace Mears Levy* (Mrs. Moses Levy), p. 19

Earl, Ralph, *Elizabeth Schuyler Hamilton*, p. 20

East River Waterfront, p. 157

Egyptian headdress and collar, p. 126

"El" Second and Third Avenue Lines, Bowery and Division Street, Manhattan, p. 178

Election Night, p. 150

11 Christopher Street, p. 134

Elias Braman, Jr., p. 24

Elizabeth Schuyler Hamilton, p. 20

Ellis Island (man reading a newspaper), p. 191

Empire State Building Construction, p. 158

Empire State Building Construction, p. 159

End of an Epoch, The, p. 184

Erie Canal Celebration, New York, p. 52

Evacuation Day jug, p. 25

Evening dress, p. 98

Fall-front desk (writing cabinet), p. 27

False Alarm, p. 162

Fan, p. 99

Fancy-dress costume: "The Spirit of Electricity," p. 98

Feinstein, Harold, *Teenagers on Coney Island Beach*, p. 190

Feist, Frances, *Louis Armstrong, Cotton Club*, p. 142

Ferry Wharves, N.Y., p. 124

Fiene, Ernest, *St. Patrick's Cathedral*, p. 197

Fifth Avenue and Eighty-ninth Street in 1868, p. 92

Figurehead of Andrew Jackson from the frigate "Constitution," p. 68

Fire at the Tombs, p. 60

Frank Work Driving a Fast Team of Trotters, p. 97

Freeman, Don, *False Alarm*, p. 162

Friedlander, Isac, *Revival*, p. 162

Front Row, p. 168

Fulton, Robert, *Self-Portrait*, p. 28

Fulton Fish Market Dock, 1934, p. 170

Gaming or tric-trac table, p. 74

Gansevoort Street No. 53, Manhattan, p. 179

Gatto, Victor Joseph, *Triangle Fire (March 25, 1911)*, pp. 138–139

George Brown Manufacturing Company, *Broadway & Fifth Avenue omnibus*, p. 121

George Gershwin at the Piano, p. 144

George Washington, p. 22

Goelet Prize for Sloops, p. 75

Goetz, Esther, *Sullivan Street*, p. 154

Goldbeck, Walter Dean, *Clifton Webb in Formal Evening Dress*, p. 145

Gordigiani, Michele, *Cornelia Ward Hall and Her Children*, pp. 100–101

Gottscho, Samuel H., *Luna Park, Coney Island*, p. 130

Gottscho-Schleisner, Inc., *Silhouette, Midtown Manhattan*, p. 156

Grace Mears Levy (Mrs. Moses Levy), p. 19

Gracie (long-face Jumeau doll), p. 30

Greyhound Bus Terminal, 244–248 West 34th Street and 245–249 West 33rd Street, Manhattan, p. 177

Grossman, Sid, *Harlem Street Scene*, p. 180; *Jitterbugging in Harlem*, p. 180

Group of Boys, p. 161

Handmade paper dolls, p. 30

Harlem Street Scene, p. 180

Harriet Ashton Clarkson Crosby (Mrs. William Bedlow Crosby), p. 83

Harris Theater, New York, p. 187

Harrison, B. J., *Annual Fair of the American Institute at Niblo's Garden*, p. 62

Harvey, George, *Nightfall, St. Thomas' Church, Broadway, New York*, p. 56

Hassam, Childe, *Rainy Late Afternoon, Union Square*, pp. 116–117; *Washington's Birthday, Fifth Avenue & Twenty-third Street*, p. 140

Healy, George P. A., *Caroline Slidell Perry* (Mrs. August Belmont, Sr.), p. 91

Hepp, August, *Central Park, Gapstow, Bridge*, p. 106; *Central Park, Boat House*, p. 107

Herrman, Augustine, *New Amsterdam (The Montanus View)*, p. 2

Hill, J.W., *Papprill View of New York*, pp. 80–81

Hill, John William, *Broadway and Rector Street*, pp. 76–77

Hine, Lewis, *Empire State Building Construction*, p. 158; *Empire State Building Construction*, p. 159

Hoffbauer, Charles Constantin Joseph, *Roof Garden (Study No. 2 for "Sur les Toits")*, p. 127

Holing Through, p. 155

Hopkins, Peter, *Riot at Union Square, March 6, 1930*, p. 152

Howard the Duck, p. 201

Humpty Dumpty circus toys, p. 123

Hunt, Richard Morris, *Leaded glass window, from the home of Henry G. Marquand*, p. 98

Hunting River Thieves, p. 110

Imbert, Anthony, *Erie Canal Celebration, New York*, p. 52

Inman, Henry, *John Carland* p. 61

Inman, John O'Brien, *Moonlight Skating—Central Park, The Lake and Terrace, 1878*, p. 93

Irvin, Rea, *Window Seat at Christmas*, p. 196

Italian Kitchen, p. 195

Jam Session, p. 143

Jarvis, John Wesley, *Philip Hone*, p. 28

Jitterbugging in Harlem, p. 180

Johanna Stoutenburgh Hone (Mrs. John Hone), p. 23

John Carland, p. 61

Justina Brandly Lasarus Isaacs (Mrs. Joshua Isaacs), p. 23

Kainen, Jacob, *Tenement Fire*, p. 163

Kanaga, Consuelo, *Tenement*, p. 181

Kelly's Alley, p. 135

Kerr, James W., *Seventh Avenue Subway*, p. 153; *Times Square Dim-Out*, p. 188

Kierstede, Cornelius, *Tankard*, p. 26

Kish, Maurice, *East River Waterfront*, p. 157; *The End of an Epoch*, p. 184

Kittell, Nicholas Biddle, *Mr. and Mrs. Charles Henry Augustus Carter*, p. 77

La Gambina, Vincent, *Life Cafeteria*, p. 167

Lace parasol with coral handle, p. 99

Landing of General Lafayette at Castle Garden, New York, August 1824, p. 53

Lane, Fitz Hugh, *Clipper Ship "Sweepstakes,"* p. 71

Lannuier, Charles-Honoré, *Gaming or tric-trac table*, p. 74

Lawrence, Richard Hoe, *Hunting River Thieves*, p. 110; *"Black and Tan" Dive in Broome St. Near Wooster St.*, p. 113; *Mullin's Alley, Cherry Hill*, p. 114

Leaded glass window, from the home of Henry G. Marquand, p. 98

LEE (Lee George Quiñones), *Howard the Duck*, p. 201

Lee, Ming Cho, *Set model for the New York City Opera Production of* Faust, p. 143

Lemon and Orange Stand, p. 58

Life Cafeteria, p. 167

Louis Armstrong, Cotton Club, p. 142

Louis Marx & Company, *Mechanical mouse "Merrymakers" band*, p. 121

Louisa Ward Crawford Terry, p. 86

Luna Park, Coney Island, p. 130

McAuliffe, John, *Frank Work Driving a Fast Team of Trotters*, p. 97

McClean, Howard, *Chinese Theater*, p. 96

McKay, L., *Steeplechase Park, Coney Island*, p. 120

MacMonnies, Frederick, *Nathan Hale*, p. 87

Man in Rain, p. 193

Manhattan Company Reservoir, pp. 52–53

Maria Burritt Cowdrey (Mrs. Peter Anderson Cowdrey), p. 24

Marsh, Reginald, *No. 6—Bowery*, p. 186; *Harris Theater, New York*, p. 187

"Mary Powell," p. 104

Mary Spratt Provoost Alexander (Mrs. James Alexander), p. 17

Maverick, Samuel, *Landing of General Lafayette at Castle Garden, New York, August 1824*, p. 53

Mead, Ginger and Root Beer Cart, The, p. 58

Mechanical mouse "Merrymakers" band, p. 121

Mehitabel Hodges ("the Salem Doll"), p. 31

Minnelli, Vincente, *Jam Session*, p. 143

Mitchell, Benn, *Chinese Hand Laundry*, p. 194; *Italian Kitchen*, p. 195

Model of the sailing ferry "Independent," p. 69

Model of the ship "Half Moon," p. 69

Moonlight Skating—Central Park, The Lake and Terrace, 1878, p. 93

Moore-Park, Carton, *Washington Square*, p. 128

Moran, Edward, *Unveiling of the Statue of Liberty*, p. 105

Moses Levy, p. 18

Mount, William Sidney, *Adelaide E. Brooks, John E. Brooks and George Spencer Brooks as Children*, p. 85

Mr. and Mrs. Charles Henry Augustus Carter, p. 77

Mr. Israel Bear Kursheedt, p. 64

Mullin's Alley, Cherry Hill, p. 114

Municipal Building, The, cover

Myers, Jerome, *Street Carousel*, p. 183

Myers, Myer, *Coffeepot*, p. 29

Nathan Hale, p. 87

New Amsterdam (The Montanus View), p. 2

New York Herald's *four-in-hand drag on Tenth Avenue between Forty-fourth and Forty-fifth Streets during the course of a city planning tour, The*, p. 133

Night School in the Seventh Avenue Lodging House, p. 112

Nightfall, St. Thomas' Church, Broadway, New York, p. 56

No. 6—Bowery, p. 186

Noah's ark, p. 121

Norman, da Loria, *Holing Through*, p. 155

Oertel, Johannes E., *Woodruff Stables*, p. 90

Olivia P. Murray Cutting (Mrs. William Bayard Cutting), p. 118

On the Alert at Bryant Park—N.Y.C., p. 185

Onckelbag, Gerrit, *Brandywine bowl*, p. 26

Open robe, p. 22

Opening Night, Ziegfeld Follies, pp. 148–149

Orkin, Ruth, *Man in Rain*, p. 193

Oudinot, E. S., *Leaded glass window, from the home of Henry G. Marquand*, p. 98

Palmer, Frances F., *American Country Life: October Afternoon*, p. 84

Pansing, Fred, *Sampson and Schley Leading the Fleet into New York Harbor, August 20, 1898*, p. 124

Papprill, Henry, *Papprill View of New York*, pp. 80–81

Papprill View of New York, pp. 80–81

Paradise Roof Garden atop Hammerstein's Victoria, p. 131

Parkes, W. S., *Crystal Palace*, p. 63

Peale, Rembrandt, *Johanna Stoutenburgh Hone (Mrs. John Hone)*, p. 23

Pearsee, Jonathan, *Card table*, p. 27

Pedestal-end sideboard, p. 74

Pennell, Joseph, *Ferry Wharves, N.Y.*, p. 124

Philip Hone, p. 28

Phyfe, Duncan, *Pedestal-end sideboard*, p. 74

Police Station Lodgers 3, Stranded in the Strange City, p. 111

Police Station Lodgers 8, A "Scrub" and Her Bed, p. 111

Queensboro Bridge, p. 164

Quiñones, Lee George (LEE), *Howard the Duck*, p. 201

Rainy Late Afternoon, Union Square, pp. 116–117

Ravlin, Grace, *Red Cross Parade, Fifth Avenue*, p. 141

Rebekah Seixas Kursheedt (Mrs. Israel Bear Kursheedt), p. 65

Red Cross Parade, Fifth Avenue, p. 141

Red Wall II, p. 200

Reisman, Philip, *Red Wall II*, p. 200

Revival, p. 162

Richard K. Haight Family, The, p. 73

Riis, Jacob A., *Hunting River Thieves*, p. 110; *Police Station Lodgers 3, Stranded in the Strange City*, p. 111; *Police Station Lodgers 8, A "Scrub" and Her Bed*, p. 111; *Night School in the Seventh Avenue Lodging House*, p. 112; *"Black and Tan" Dive in Broome St. Near Wooster St.*, p. 113; *Mullin's Alley, Cherry Hill*, p. 114

Riot at Union Square, March 6, 1930, p. 152

Robert Fulton, *Self-Portrait*, p. 28

Rocking horse, p. 122

Rohowsky, Meyers, *On the Alert at Bryant Park—N.Y.C.*, p. 185

Roof Garden (Study No. 2 for "Sur les Toits"), p. 127

Roof Garden, Madison Square Garden Theatre, p. 132

Rosenberg, Charles G., *Wall Street, Half Past 2 o'Clock, October 13, 1857*, p. 89

"Royal" pattern champagne glasses, p. 126

Safranek, Doug, *Still Open*, p. 199

St. Patrick's Cathedral, p. 197

Sampson and Schley Leading the Fleet into New York Harbor, August 20, 1898, p. 124

Set model for the New York City Opera Production of Faust, p. 143

Seventh Avenue Subway, p. 153

Shanks, Ann Zane, *Date Night: Saturday Night on the Third Avenue El*, p. 192

Sheppard, Warren, *Brooklyn Bridge Celebration, May 1883*, p. 102

Side chair, p. 27

Silhouette, Midtown Manhattan, p. 156

Simmon, Rudolph, *Busy Intersection with Trolley Cars and Elevated Railroad*, p. 160; *Group of Boys*, p. 161

Simonson, James Brownlee, *The Back Parlor* (Bianchi residence), p. 95

Sir (Cyril Ritchard), p. 142

Sixth Avenue North from Forty-seventh Street, p. 172

Sloan, John, *Snowstorm in the Village*, p. 150

Smith, Henry Pember, *The Columbian Parade, Washington Square, 1892*, p. 119

Snowstorm in the Village, p. 150

Soble, John J., *Sixth Avenue North from Forty-seventh Street*, p. 172

Sonntag, W. Louis, Jr., *The Brooklyn Bridge*, p. 103; *Bowery at Night*, p. 125

S. S. "Normandie" First Class, Grand Salon Looking Forward, p. 165

Steeplechase Park, Coney Island, p. 120

Steichen, Edward, *Bryant Park Breadline*, p. 174

Stettheimer, Carrie Walter, *Stettheimer Doll House*, pp. 146–147

Stettheimer Doll House, pp. 146–147

Still Open, p. 199

Stone, Erika, *Ellis Island* (man reading a newspaper), p. 191

Storefront Mission, Brooklyn, p. 173

Storm over Manhattan, p. 182

Street Carousel, p. 183

Stuart, Gilbert, *George Washington*, p. 22

Suba, Miklos, *Storefront Mission, Brooklyn*, p. 173

"Subway" presentation tray, p. 75

Sullivan Street, p. 154

Tankard, p. 26

Teddy bear, p. 122

Teenagers on Coney Island Beach, p. 190

Temples of God and Gold, p. 151

Tenement, p. 181

Tenement Fire, p. 163

Thain, Howard A., *Opening Night, Ziegfeld Follies*, pp. 148–149

Thomas D. Rice Performing His "Jump Jim Crow" Routine at the American Theatre, Bowery, N.Y., November 25, 1833, p. 59

Thompson, C. G., *Mr. Israel Bear Kursheedt*, p. 64; *Rebekah Seixas Kursheedt (Mrs. Israel Bear Kursheedt)*, p. 65

Tiffany, Louis Comfort, *Egyptian headdress and collar*, p. 126

Tiffany & Company, *Goelet Prize for Sloops*, p. 75; *"Subway" presentation tray*, p. 75

Tiffany Glass and Decorating Company, *"Royal" pattern champagne glasses*, p. 126

Tiffany Studios, *Two-part vase*, p. 126

Times Square Dim-Out, p. 188

Triangle Fire (March 25, 1911), pp. 138–139

Two-part vase, p. 126

Union Square, pp. 54–55

Unveiling of the Statue of Liberty, p. 105

Valley Grove Tavern, Entrance to Port Road, Prospect Park, Brooklyn, p. 94

Van Brunt, James R., *Valley Grove Tavern, Entrance to Port Road, Prospect Park, Brooklyn*, p. 94

Velonis, Anthony, *Fulton Fish Market Dock, 1934*, p. 170

View of Hudson River, p. 70

View of New York from Staten Island, pp. 66–67

View of New York, Brooklyn and the Navy Yard from the Heights near Williamsburg, p. 72

View northeast from the roof of George Ehret's home at Park Avenue and Ninety-fourth Street, p. 109

View southwest from the roof of George Ehret's home at Park Avenue and Ninety-fourth Street, p. 108

Vista from West Street, p. 176

V-J Day, Times Square (study), p. 189

Waldo, Samuel Lovett, *Harriet Ashton Clarkson Crosby* (Mrs. William Bedlow Crosby), p. 83

Walker, Izannah, *Cloth doll*, p. 31

Wall Street, Half Past 2 o'Clock, October 13, 1857, p. 89

Ward, John Quincy Adams, *August Belmont, Sr.*, p. 86

Warehouse, Water and Dock Streets, Brooklyn, p. 177

Warner, Everett, *The Municipal Building*, cover

Washington Square, p. 128

Washington's Birthday, Fifth Avenue & Twenty-third Street, p. 140

Waugh, Samuel B., *The Bay and Harbor of New York*, p. 78

Werner, Anna Goth, *The Crematory* (Fresh Pond Crematory, Ridgewood, Queens), p. 198

Willett, Marinus, *Card table*, p. 27

William Cumbel and Eliza Kate Wilson, p. 82

Window Seat at Christmas, p. 196

Winter Scene in Brooklyn, pp. 50–51

Wittop, Freddy, *Sir (Cyril Ritchard)*, p. 142

Wollaston, John, *Mary Spratt Provoost Alexander* (Mrs. James Alexander), p. 17

Woodruff Stables, p. 90

Worth/Paris, *Evening dress*, p. 98; *Fancy-dress costume: "The Spirit of Electricity,"* p. 98

Wuxtry (Newsboy), p. 169

Yachting in New York Harbor, p. 70

Yavno, Max, *Big City Playground*, p. 181

Zorach, William, *Builders of the Future*, p. 166

Our Town, Images and Stories from the Museum of the City of New York was edited and produced by Constance Sullivan and Peter Simmons. The book was designed by Katy Homans who also set the type. Peter Simmons, with Joanna Ellwood, coordinated the project and facilitated editorial preparation. Julie DeWitt was associate picture editor. Ellyn Allison copyedited the text. Robert Hennessey provided advice on printing the duotone illustrations. Separations were made and printing realized in Hong Kong, through Palace Press International, New York.